Travels with Honey

A Modern-Day Pilgrimage, A Gift of Love

Bess Miles-Duncan

BALBOA PRESS

A DIVISION OF HAY HOUSE

ISBN: 978-1-4525-5369-6 (sc)
ISBN: 978-1-4525-5371-9 (e)
ISBN: 978-1-4525-5370-2 (hc)

Library of Congress Control Number: 2012910625

Balboa Press books may be ordered through booksellers or by contacting:

Balboa Press
A Division of Hay House
1663 Liberty Drive
Bloomington, IN 47403
www.balboapress.com
1-(877) 407-4847

Because of the dynamic nature of the Internet, any web addresses or links contained in this book may have changed since publication and may no longer be valid. The views expressed in this work are solely those of the author and do not necessarily reflect the views of the publisher, and the publisher hereby disclaims any responsibility for them.

The author of this book does not dispense medical advice or prescribe the use of any technique as a form of treatment for physical, emotional, or medical problems without the advice of a physician, either directly or indirectly. The intent of the author is only to offer information of a general nature to help you in your quest for emotional and spiritual well-being. In the event you use any of the information in this book for yourself, which is your constitutional right, the author and the publisher assume no responsibility for your actions.

Any people depicted in stock imagery provided by Thinkstock are models, and such images are being used for illustrative purposes only. Certain stock imagery © Thinkstock.

Printed in the United States of America

Balboa Press rev. date: 07/05/12

This book is dedicated
to my lovely husband and wonderful dog,
and to all my friends who helped me on my way.
I hope to give some of the proceeds from
this book will be able to go to
charities for creatures not as lucky as Honey.

Honey for those who do not her is a lurcher. Lurchers
are now seen as a breed by Crufts in England. She
is part Bedlington Terrier and part whippet which
makes her an unique but lovely creature. At the
start of the journey she is 18 months old and on her
passport she is coloured brindle.She is also very fast.

Travels with Honey

ANDALUCIA

Some days you go to the shops and come home and settle down to read a good book and nothing takes shape but the simplicity of life. So why change it and fling yourself into foreign travel? To so many people staying safe would be more important. I am not sure I know what the answer is, but off we went hoping to see what it was like to live in Europe during the winter. Others had done it before, so why not us? We found a place to stay in Spain on the Internet and inquired if they took small dogs. They said they did, so we thought we would have an adventure. Life can seem very short or very long depending upon your perspective, and Howard, my husband of less than a year had never been on any of these crazy adventures.. So he was all for it.

I booked our place on the ferry and rang three removal companies to check out who would be best to look after our furniture. Some of my pieces had been manhandled in and out of furniture trucks for years and so were getting quite used to the experience. The trouble is that it never seems to get any easier. We had plenty of time to pack and sort things out using free cycle and the charity shops in and around our home area and to start to learn Spanish. Now and again my stress levels started to go up a gear when on top of that Honey came into season. I believe no dog has been so protected from the male of the species. I so wish I had been as carefully watched. Every time she went outside Howard or I would be there to make sure she did not get tampered with. It was a grueling fortnight, or would have been if she had not gotten into hunting. She seemed more interested in staring at various parts of the garden and standing for hours hoping to catch something. Thank goodness the next-door dog, Jake, did not catch her. I would not like to have been stuck in Spain with a litter of puppies too.

Before we set off I had to get the car a MOT, In England a M.O.T., Ministry of Transport test is required for cars over four years old and if that was not enough stress, my ex died. I think if I had not used meditation and the Alexandre technique I would have been carried away or put on strong tranquilizers before the voyage of discovery, but somehow I seemed to get through it. We had planned to stay with my mother-in-law for a few days so we could clean our empty house. Was this going to be another stress? Actually, it was a joy except that there was no Internet available. A few things needed sorting out so I had to go to the library in town to use the internet. My mother-in-law made us totally at home and was really helpful in making sure we were fed after a hard day's cleaning. Our leaving for Europe coincided, too, with the death of a close friend, in fact my ex of many years. His death seemed to clear the way for us to go, as he had not enjoyed life for what seemed a long time and was going downhill rapidly. None of it is pleasant to witness when you care for someone, but there was nothing we could to do make life easier for him as much as we wanted to; it was totally out of our hands. We had given away our hens and said good-bye to the wood for the time being by making a memorial garden and planting an oak tree for our friend and for my mother a small fir that had been stuck in a pot for years. The whole thing was beautiful; it did what his funeral did not and was just in the right part of the wood, close to the road leading to his favorite pub. It seemed crazy to be doing that in the middle of all the cleaning we were doing, but it made perfect sense to us and added something that was needed from both lives. We were also able to place there a log we had brought from Ireland. It looked just like a seat for the little people that had travelled with it and surely now they could look after this space? Howard had a tree our friend thought would never grow and so it was placed there too, now grown to a good size. I also had a lavender and a rosemary that needed a home, and as rosemary is for remembrance it went there too. It was just perfect.

Originally we were going to stay with a friend of mine near Bristol so we could take our time getting to the ferry. This arrangement fell apart, so new arrangements were made and we decided to explore a bit and eventually left Harrogate for Stow-in-the-Wold. I had booked a hotel that takes dogs, so Honey got to see the historic town and have a decent place to stay for the night. She is fine at traveling and new places, so it was not a problem. The main trick to this way of traveling is to have plenty of plastic bags for any little piles she might leave around the ancient streets. All went well with this arrangement, and we had a pleasant evening, but unfortunately we could not get on the Internet to arrange our next place for Sunday evening. We had not booked everything up front, as we were not sure how long we wanted to stay in each place. Stow was okay but not worth another night, so we set off further south. Around Bradford upon Avon we embarked on another stop. We thought about Bath, but it looked worn, a gentle, run-down, shabby kind of place. We stopped for lunch and asked the woman behind the bar if she knew of anywhere, and she found us a lovely bed and breakfast with good walks for Honey. The owner will always stay with us in our hearts, as we loved his eccentricity. He at least had WIFI, and I was able to book a place near the ferry. Thank goodness we had made those arrangements, because getting into Portsmouth was horrendous, all roads meeting and forming massive queues. My patience was tested to the limit. My original idea of going to my sister's before going to the ferry could have meant we missed it. We did go and see my sister but on Monday rather on Tuesday, the day of embarkation. Thank goodness we gave ourselves an extra day. Honey is great at traveling, so all she does is rest and wait for freedom again.

Our next stay was in a smart hotel. While we were eating we did not leave her in a strange hotel bedroom but put her back in the car where she knows what is what.

The meal there was excellent, beautifully set out and a real treat. The hotel was rather cold and modern, but it did mean that we were near the ferry and so there was less stress during that part of the journey.

Off to the ferry we went the next day. First we wandered by the sea for a while and then got to the ferry very early so as not to be stuck in traffic again. Honey was going in a kennel, something she has never experienced, and we were given priority for getting on. She was taken to the kennel and left. It was horrible for us all, but we were issued a card so we could visit when we wanted and walk her near the helipad. One time when we were walking her with a few other dogs one large dog cocked its leg over the side onto the deck below. We did not get to see if any passengers were underneath at the time, but it did make us smile. Putting Honey back in the cage each time was horrible. She did not take to this arrangement. Even with a blanket and food she felt very miserable, so we were glad when we reached Spain. For us the trip had not been too bad. Honey survived, and we left the ferry in the dark. There had been delays through various passengers being taken off by helicopter. We were up on the top when we arrived so we could see Spain from the boat. It was a lovely experience looking down on the new land. It took a long time to get off the ferry. Passengers were allowed to get their dogs first and take them to the car. The problem was that we kept getting lost and could not find the car. For a while we were up and down staircases and in and out of lifts, each staircase looking just like the other with seemingly nobody knowing the way, even a steward working on the boat. In the end I took matters into my own hands and got over the panic and we found our way to the car. We were even delayed getting off for some reason, so it was dark when I finally drove off the ferry. I drove into Spain thinking I was going one way, but in fact I was going west instead of south. When we realized we were lost, we found a place to stay and wait for the morning, but they did not take dogs. The place I had booked was far away, and there was no way we were going to be able to get there that night. I just had to rest, as we could not go any further. Honey at least knew the car and managed a night by herself. I made myself a bit of a wreck worrying about her just like Ireland but not quite as bad as there. I had to trust that all would be well. The next morning after coffee and some cake we set off to find the right road. It was a lovely morning, and we realized our mistake. The sea and mountains looked splendid, so there was a kind of excitement as we tried to find our way south. We were now officially on our holidays. I have driven in France, Greece, and America on the right-hand side, so this was not a problem. The sun was shining and Honey was okay. What could be better?

We traveled through Toledo and further down before stopping again and caught up bit by bit on the distance we had lost the night before. This time we found a hotel on the edge of town so we could park the car in safety, as it was filled with all our belongings and our lovely dog. She was walked around some rather ugly places, but she did get a walk and seemed fine. I tried not to worry about her left in the vehicle, as she seemed well happy with these arrangements after the horror of the ferry. We kept going. The next night she could stay with us. The place was a bit strange and not really to my liking, but at least the dog was with us. Today we would reach our destination, our home in Andalucía. We got there and sent a message to our host. She replied that she had gone out to lunch and would not be there till seven. It was Saturday, and I realized that the shops would be shut early, as it was a Catholic place, and that there was even less chance of food the next day. There was not a lot to be done. There had been no supermarket on our travels that day either, so we just had to wait and see. The host finally arrived in the small town of Ugijar, and we got back into the car to follow her to our new home. I was tired by now and was suddenly driving up a mountain road with a very long drop on one side. It was hell, and I was very tired and very frightened. The woman in front of us was used to it. I was not and had the car piled high with stuff. The other side of me was rock, and it looked just as treacherous as the fall on my side. I took a deep breath and continued. Where the hell was I going?

I ended up in a small hamlet called Las Canteras in the mountains of Andalucía. It looked really interesting in the fading light. I tried to steady my shaking body from what had just happened and calm down. We were loaned a wheelbarrow to transport our things to the house. It was a lovely house built into the land with seven rooms going up and up to the balcony off the main bedroom. We dropped our bags to take a look round. We then took our lovely Honey to show her our new home as we tried to get used to the amazing scenery all around us. Our host loaned us some pasta and a few other things so I could at least make a meal. There was a big stove in the kitchen and many lovely pots and paintings about. Somehow I got it all together and we were able to sit down to eat a tuna and pasta meal and have a drink with it. We were now in such a different world from what we had left. The weather was still warm, and the house had been built to keep the place as cool as possible. It was painted white just for that purpose. We were exhausted from all the traveling and fell into the big bed at the top of the house very soon after the meal. I lay there wondering about my fear and shock at the journey up the mountain. It was something I had not known, because basically I had never had to do such a thing before. In the past I had not really been upset by looking down, but that could be because most of the time I had been standing on my own two feet and not riding in a vehicle. I had walked in the Grand Canyon and not experienced a fear of falling from the heights. I had to learn to drive up and down the mountain road if we were going to make this our home. Having those thoughts I was able to fall asleep.

Held by the mountains
Sunkissed
In the morning light
We sit among it all
Shimmering in its glory.

Upon waking to the new day I walked out onto the balcony and stared at the distant mountains. It was Sunday morning and I was not going to go anywhere but just enjoy the views and find my way around. Somehow with the sleep my sense of humor had come back and the fear was not taking me over. I started to undo the bags and make this place a home, spreading our things about and getting out my books and putting out clothes onto hangers so maybe some of the wrinkles would disappear. The light was fantastic, as was the heat. There we were in October, and yet I did not need to wear loads of clothes. Honey got to walk out and discover her new surroundings. She had to go down to the bottom of the house to get out and would sit by the door to let me know she needed to wander. The path was dusty, and there was often a little dog outside called Frodo, a new little friend to get to know. My legs ached, though, because I was not used to climbing such steep steps and so many. It was all learning, finding my way around a new house and being able to wash the clothes we had dragged around with us over the last few days. There was a washer in the bathroom. Somehow I got it to work and then had to go right to the top of the house to get the clothing on the line to dry in the very hot sun.

There was a certain kind of peace to it all; it felt like we were being held by the mountains. The incredible beauty and the quiet meant you could have been there at any point of time; yet the terraces with the olives meant it had to have been after the Moors invaded the place. The river gurgled in the bottom, and the flowers set it off as much as the prickly pears. I marveled at my new space, the day before drifting off into memory and the sun on my body. I was starting to feel different, as we all were. It was a good Sunday, and I even made a kind of dhal for tea.

On Monday I took again to the mountain road to get over my fears and found I could do it if I went very slowly and did a lot of deep breathing. It took a lot of concentration, but it was worth it, as we could at last get stocked up and look around our new area. On the way down we saw mountain hares, which was exciting. I suddenly found I was out of contact with people, as none of my phones appeared to be working and I could not get WIFI. It felt odd not being able to get in touch. There was a massive TV and some kind of dish, but it did not always work well. I picked up a book to read, *Off the Road*, a book by the wife of Neal Cassady, telling the tale of her marriage and friendship with Jack Kerouac. It seemed the right book to read, as we were definitely on the road and I noticed the similarities of our lives and our choice of men.

The house martins hold us in awe
As they dance in the fading light
To the fly opera
Goats had started off the evening
Ringing their bells
Sun dipping behind the mountain
The moon graced us with its presence
And the dew drifted in
Cooling us down for the nighttime revelry
The curtains closed with the dark
And we were left with the stars once more.

The next day I did not bother to drive anywhere. I had done enough driving over the last week, and it was good to just take in the new sights and smells. The heat was something else; we could only stay out for shorts snippets of time even though it was October. When it cooled down I took Honey for a walk to the river running through the mountains and found wild fennel and mint growing. We all enjoyed ourselves that day, especially with the house martins giving us another lovely display before bedtime as we watched the sun go down over the mountains.

On Wednesday there was a market in the local town, so we wandered back down the mountain and took a look at it all. Howard bought a new shirt, and I tried getting on the Internet. There were so many e-mails—a lot of rubbish, so a lot to delete. In the end the machine just could not do it all. It was so old and well used I could not properly see some of the letters. When we went back to the village I was thrilled to see red peppers being dried in the sun. They looked great with the deep red against the white-washed houses. The next day our host took me down to where I should be able to get on the Internet again, but again the connection was poor. The weather and the peace made up for it, and I tried to get over the ease with which I was able to find out things before when we had broadband.

Each day we give Honey more freedom to roam around the village. At least around there the cars could not go fast, but she still dashed up to strangers to say "Hello." They did not understand such a dog with that much zest for life. I rushed up to them and dragged her off. I continued with my book, which did not move on so much while Howard read four books. It was interesting, though, reading the lives of people who probably changed our view of things.

We continued to marvel at the views around us, staring into the distance and trying to take it all in. I loved the sounds too—the bird song and the goats wandering about, only showing they were there by of the bells around their necks. Even with the binoculars I could not focus on them, but in time I would. I seemed to be getting better at relaxing and just taking things bit by bit; this place seemed good for me.

One evening I walked up the mountain instead of down with Honey. I was curious and found the walk exhilarating. It was good to look down at the houses and have everything seem far away. Suddenly Honey went off the track, and next thing I knew she had her nose next to a beehive. She got stung and rolled about in the clay soil. I realized that I could have been at risk if she had upset them all, as I am allergic to bee stings. There I was with no way of phoning that I was stung. The thought of that happening with the phones not working well reminded me how at risk I was in that place. Luckily I did not panic but took my scarf and tied it round her collar to get her back down the mountain safely. I was reminded of the warning I got and decided to think things through more.

The next day we took a trip to Berja, but it felt empty on the way back, as if the day was wasted. I still could not find a satisfactory place to sort out my accounts and bills and felt in limbo. I start Jean Houston's book *The Goddess and the Hero* and looked at the idea of pilgrimage and metaphor. It helped me back to myself, and I grew calm again. The other problem we were having was that the fiesta was nearly upon us and we needed lots of provisions, as all the shops were shut. Our host seemed unreliable; she kept changing dates, and we were unsure what to do. We decided to make an early start the next day and see what we could buy to keep us going.

It was a lovely morning with perfect blue skies as we made our way hopefully along the mountain road. I was starting to feel a little better about it when all of a sudden there was a bang and a rattle and a piece of our vehicle flung itself onto the road. I gazed back it and shut off the engine. The part was smoking, so I got out to take a look. Howard had not realized the enormity of it, and as soon as he did he joined me. We stared at the part for a while wondering what to do next. As there were no passing places next to us we got an old bag from the car and moved the boiling part to the side of the road. Howard backed the vehicle to the nearest passing place. There was nothing to do but to make our way back to the house. Luckily we had not gone very far and so the journey was not too bad. The sun was already warming up the place. It would have been a very uncomfortable journey up the hill if we had gone too far and it happened. It was all uphill from where we were as we trudged back with our things. I tried not to panic and went to find my info on the RAC, a company in England that provided roadside aid for cars, I had brought with me. We had little money on our phones now—we seemed unable to find anywhere to get them sorted out, as anybody ringing us would add to our own bill. Luckily I managed to get through and was told that they would help me get the car off the mountain and to a garage. The other problem we had was not only was it fiesta time but it was also a bank holiday. We did not expect anything to happen that day and so made the most of the few things we had left in the house for drinks and to eat. Suddenly there was a shouting and we realized that a man and a tow truck were waiting for us to get the key to the vehicle so he could take it away. He was in a very bad mood, probably because he had not wanted to work on a bank holiday. Our neighbor spoke to him but could not get much more sense than we had. I never expected to see the vehicle again. I remained reasonably calm, coming to the conclusion that there was nothing really we could do about it. It was done, and we had to make the most of things. Of course it was the worst thing that it some ways could have happened, as were stuck up a mountain with little food and drink and there was certainly no bus service this far away from the larger communities in the valley. Someone offered to take us down with them the next day to get some food if we were up for nine thirty. As we could not be choosers, as they say of beggars, we would try that. We were going to get a hire car at some point too, but first we had to get down the mountain before we could do anything else. It was a case of waiting and being patient. I started to wonder about the merit of *The Goddess and the Hero*. I was not sure I wanted adventures. They all seemed too hard. But then it was a huge test of faith, and I was definitely being tested. Oh dear!

In the evening I wandered down to the river again with Honey and enjoyed the quiet gurgling of the river and the vastness of the mountains before me. It was a beautiful place. I loved rock and stone and the ruggedness of it all but then was reminded that there was a price for this beauty, and I was paying it. Sometimes we are aware of the choice we are making when we chose beauty over practicality. The olive trees and the orange trees were held by the landscape formed around us. I managed to feed us and have a pleasant evening even if yet again I was struggling with vehicles that did not always work when you wanted them to. I suppose if I looked at the cup-half-full or the cup-half-empty view of things, then my small breakdowns were nothing, as the vehicle worked most of the time. I think it was the abruptness of it all. One moment you are moving on in your life and then next moment it is all go slow or stop. I checked to see if it was another sign, something I might be missing or denying in my life, but then with the book I was reading concluded that it was part of the adventure.

The next day we were up for our trip to the town to get food, taken by a couple from the village. We sat in the square and waited, but then there was a phone call from the RAC to tell us that we would be taken for the hire car today by taxi. We thanked the couple and waited for the taxi. It eventually arrived, but the driver would not let the dog go. I ran back to the house to see if Lucinda , our neighbour, would look after Honey, but she was fast asleep. So not to delay anything more I decided to leave Honey with Howard and go alone with the taxi driver to pick up the hire car. I had everything I needed in the handbag and so jumped into the waiting taxi, waving as we went back down the mountain. The driver was a pleasant chap who spoke some English, so I was able to converse a little and keep off the apprehension that was beginning to take over. I was seated in the back and so could see around me and the long fall if the car went over. The taxi driver took it all in his stride and would turn to chat now and again. Over and over again I told to myself with positive statements that all would be well and I would be safe. We made our way via Berja and toward the sea. Would I ever be seen again? I was alone with a strange man in a strange land and had no idea where I was going. We passed a fascinating house. I was sure it was the home of a real eccentric, and then I saw in the distance, a sea of plastic. It was backdropped against the Mediterranean, one sea after the other, one completely ugly and the other a beautiful blue. I tried to come to terms with it. What a way to grow crops, and what would it be like to work in the awful place? They employed loads of people from abroad, but what was it costing the earth? How much water was being used to keep us with tomatoes and melons all year round?

I talked about it with the taxi driver, and he mentioned how unusually hot it was in Spain this year. He said that it was never as hot in October as this and was obviously worried about it all. There had hardly been any rain either. I asked him if he thought it was global warming, but he did not reply. Eventually we were in the middle of the plastic, shed after shed or greenhouse after greenhouse of crops, all looking the same. It was a horrible and frightening experience, because if you got lost in this sea of plastic there were no signposts to find your way out. He advised me not come back that way. It brought up many questions, about housing and transport for the workers, safety, and what it meant to the locals who live in the area. Abruptly it stopped, and I was suddenly in a town that could have been in America or Mexico, anywhere they provided people with large hotels and palm trees, an enormous contrast to the plastic city I had just been through. This was where the hire car place was situated, and he waited for me to see if there was anybody there. They might have gone off to lunch, but there was a woman waiting for me. I went back outside, and the taxi drive drove off. I was now alone in this weird area and completed the form and took the keys to the next vehicle I would be driving. I thought I'd better get a drink before I set off and go to the loo. The woman who handed me the key to the car told me which way to go and mentioned that there was a supermarket nearby. I wandered in to get some food for our tea. I was a shaking wreck and tried to calm myself. I bought a few things and went to find the car. It seemed very big compared to our truck, and of course I now had to drive sitting on the other side of the car. I maneuvered it out of the car park with difficulty just as a truck was coming in that would not know that this was the first time I had driven the car and needed time to find my way about it. So now I was driving in a town I did not know with a car I did not know and was not sure which way I should go to get back to my husband and dog. I drove slowly to get used to it and got through the streets somehow. I followed signs for the main Spanish highway but lost them eventually and ended up outside a bar where I stopped for a coffee and the loo. I tried to make people understand that I was lost and needed directions, but both people I spoke to seemed unable to help. I drove on only to turn round yet again and again before I found a road into the hills and mountains, which must mean I was going north. After being high up in the truck the car seemed very low down, and now I had no cushion and so was worried about scratching the car's sides in that position. Yet through more busy streets and little towns I edged my way north and back to where I had come from. I do not know how I did it. I was really scared of scratching the car, and some streets seemed so narrow. I finally got to Berja but got lost in the back streets, my hands holding tightly to the wheel and my mouth full of anguish, cursing the situation I was in. Finally I recognized the way out and quickly took it getting back on to the road to Ugijar. I drove through the mountains and found the road to our house. The road was really terrifying in this car, made for slick streets, not mountain roads with no give on either side. Again I found my way up into the village or hamlet and parked. I met a van coming the other way, and there I was pushed into the side of the mountain with a man shouting at me. I could not understand a word he said, and he did he not understand that I was new to all this and especially to driving this car. As you can imagine, when I arrived there I was a complete wreck only to be told by the RAC that I had to go back to the place I came from the next day and sign a document to say I wanted the car looked at by the garage. Somehow we got a meal together that night but decided to not to even try to come back with this vehicle. We decided we would stay away for some days until we could get our own car back and so not have to travel the difficult route up and down the mountain. It was just too much for me with such an expensive vehicle at my disposal. I did not want to be responsible, and traveling backward and forward from the coast to this place was not pleasant. We decided to go to Nerja. The travel book said it was interesting, and it sounded like our kind of place. We packed our bags and took the route back down the mountain in the morning. I got it down in one piece and headed for the place I tried so hard to get out of the day before. Why could I have not signed the form yesterday when I was there? It was too late now to change that so back to the coast I went with the dog and my lovely husband. He managed to see the garage as we drove in. It is so much easier when there are two of you. I drove to the end of the road and turned at a roundabout, and we went back on ourselves to the garage. My vehicle was parked outside, so I went in to inquire about what to do next. The girl behind the desk did not understand anything I said. We both talked to each other and got nowhere. There were some men talking outside; luckily one spoke a little English and became my interpreter. I signed the document, and we made our way for the coastal route. It made for a change, and we enjoyed the journey in some ways. It did seem a long way, but eventually we stopped for some lunch and stared at the sea as we ate. It was good to leave the car for a while and just relax.

Nerja was not remotely like we expected. We wandered around with the dog and felt more and more upset that it did not meet our expectations. Even though the guidebook had said that they had hotels that took dogs, we got turned away over and over again. We did find an Internet café where I was able to look at a few e-mails after all the time the privilege had been denied to me. We needed a roof for the night and to settle down after the last few days, which had been so

17

stressful. There was no room at the inn. We had even walked
back across the town in the searing sun to a hotel that said
it had Internet and again were turned away. We were tired,
hot, and basically at the end of our tether. It was all too much,
but we got back into the car and went our way back toward
the way we came. We found another seaside town and drove
through it at the busiest part of the day as it was getting dark.
I had to do something; suddenly I found a square by the sea
with a sweet hotel in the corner. I stopped and parked the car
and walked over to see if we could stay the night. It seemed a
safe place to leave the car and the dog if they would not take
Honey. It had everything we needed: there was a man who
spoke English and helped me with the parking tickets, and
they had WIFI. This we found a much better place than the
one we had left and smaller and easier to get around. We could
take Honey for a walk by the sea. She was not allowed on the
beach, but it was a pleasant walk and she could meet lots of
other dogs as we went our way. Having WIFI made life so
much easier, as I was able to get on top of all my e-mails and
attend to things I could not do in an Internet café. It took a
lot of worry away, as I was not able to sort things any other
way when I was so far from home—not that we had a proper
home anymore with the mad journey we had undertaken.

We made the most of being near the Mediterranean and
walked only a few yards from our hotel to a restaurant on the
beach. It was perfect there. We had paella especially made
for us and toasted ourselves with good wine. It was a lovely
experience and was just what needed after all the stress of
the last few days. We decided to spend another day there, as
it was so nice, and have some quality time just wandering.
Honey was safe in the back of the car and slept very well. I
prayed that she be looked after and tried not to worry about

the little dog we so loved. The next morning we got up early and took her for another walk and got ourselves a coffee and watched all the joggers and early-morning people take their constitutional. It was good fun, and I could feel my sense of humor come back.

We went back to the hotel for breakfast, and then I moved the car down the street to where I did not have to pay and was able to leave it all day until we put Honey back in it at night. Then I took it back to where we had it the night before. We spent a lovely day wandering around the town and sampling various tapas, and I treated myself to a little skirt and top. I felt a lot better, but we heard that we could not pick the car up till Wednesday, so we had a few more days to wait. It was going to cost around £700, and we could only pick it up on Wednesday night. There seemed nothing much else we could do but say yes. This was the weekend, so on Monday we would have to go back to the garage and sign yet another piece of paper to say we would pay all that money for the repair of the vehicle.

That night we ate again in the same restaurant as the night before but they had a change of waiter and it was not as good. Yet it was a lovely place to sit and watch the sea.

The next day was Sunday, so we moved further down the coast. We had seen a doggy hotel not far away and so made for there. The unfortunate thing was that nobody seemed to know where it was. I drove round and round the town, at one point getting stuck up a street that seemed to be going skyward and the wrong way. Howard had to rescue me as I panicked, and we got to flat roads again. Eventually we got pointed out of town, but still we could not see it. There was a large hotel in front of us. I was tired of driving so much again and needed to stop. It was getting hot, and we seemed destined to be always on the road. I made my way to it and found us another room for the night. This time Honey could stay in their car park.

The hotel was massive. Perched on a cliff, it overlooked the sea from the other direction from which we had been seen it the night before. We had to laugh to ourselves at the bizarreness of it all. But at least we had a roof over our heads for another night. They served a buffet lunch, and to quiet my nerves, which is my way, I went for some lunch. The evening meal was served so much later in Spain, so I thought it the best plan of action. I walked into a busy dining room. There seemed nobody about to tell me where to sit, so I took a plate and wandered around the assortment of food and got some salad and some pasta. The pasta was like baby food and gave me a kind of nurtured feeling after such a traumatic morning. It all tasted good, and I felt very strange sitting there with all those people who seemed to know what they were doing. Most were from bus trips and so knew each other, but I did not know that at that stage. I wandered out feeling oh such much better. Our room was high up with a balcony that did not seem all that safe but would do the trick; from there you could see the sea and a windy road down to a beach. Later on when it was cooler we took Honey for a walk down this road. She seemed fine in the car and behaved very well. Perhaps she understood our dilemma. We enjoyed the walks with her down the roads behind the hotel and at one point bumped into a Christopher Lee–type character with his beautiful boyfriend. They had their dogs and admired Honey with all her beauty. As we got lower and closer to the sea there was a terrible smell, which could have been many human bodies for all we knew. We joked that the hotel was a lure and all the old people on the coaches ended up down there. The road to the beach was a long one and too long for the time, but nevertheless we admired it all and wondered what it would be like to live in one of the very smart houses or should I say mansions nearby. We went to take Honey some food in the evening and found that she had stood on the alarm system of the car and the lights were flashing on and off. Trust our dog to do something like that! She got yet another walk around the well-lit hotel, but we covered anything in the car she could press with her feet.

That night we ate well and were even provided with a bottle of wine on our table, and the next morning we continued to dine superbly. Imagine my surprise when the bill for us both eating and staying in the hotel for the night was only £48.00. Surely it must be a mistake, or perhaps that was the lure for all those old people who came to see Spain. I was very tired and missed the flamenco entertainment that was put on for them too.

We had to go back and sign yet another document, so we went back the way we came and found the garage easily this time. Rather than go west again we felt that the best thing to do was to find somewhere to stay close by and so drove east along the Med. We finally found a very strange place that seemed like a ghost town. At one large hotel I approached the check-in desk to see if they had rooms and they looked at me strangely and told me they were closed for the season. Yet we did find one, and there was a garage-type cover for the car, which meant that it was even better to leave Honey in there and she would not be disturbed by light or prying eyes. This time we were given a suite for a very cheap price with plenty of waste ground for her walks. We saw a hoopoe looking for food in the wide-open spaces between road and hotels. It was so odd walking about and hardly seeing another human being except other hotel guests. I bought a very cheap swimming costume, which suited me better than my expensive one that I had forgotten to pack. Of course I had no idea when I set out that I would be staying in places that had swimming pools. I went for a quick dip in my new costume. There also seemed only one street with shops, which was odd given the large space the town occupied. We had a drink there, and they seemed to wonder why we were there. At night on our travels with Honey there was a game of tennis going on. She was fascinated by it, watching the ball being hit from one person to the next. We had to tear her away. Because of its suitability for her and the fact that it was close to our own car we asked if we could stay another night. The receptionist replied, "If you would really like to." It was as if they did not expect anyone at that type of year and there must be something wrong with you if you took them up and stayed. The food was not as good as the other hotel and was more like a canteen. We watched others pile their plates with lots of food; it seemed to bring out the greed in people to see food set up in this way. No bottle of wine there.

Our days there did not go off badly, and we were able to use the Internet to find a doggy hotel in Roquet de la Mar where the car was. Hopefully they would let Honey in when we got there. Being able to use the Internet was so useful when you could get on it. So many places advertised it, but when you got to your room it hardly ever worked. It was frustrating, but at least this hotel provided a service we could use.

It was very quiet and very strange, but looking back it could have been a lot worse. At least there were good walking areas for Honey and she was safe; that helped us feel a whole lot better too. The hotel in Roquet was horrible, not our type at all, but at least we could have Honey in the bedroom. The only good thing about the hotel was that it was on the street where I had to leave the hire car so there was no need for taxis or getting lost. I just drove it to the parking area where I had picked it up and dropped the keys off in the designated hotel. We were now carless until the evening. It was very hot, but we made our way reasonably easily to the hotel area and wandered about in the heat looking around at the various tourist shops and cafés. There was a pool area, but again dogs were not allowed in it. I had to wait till around seven to collect the car. Honey could not go in a taxi without a cage, so I had to leave the others to collect the car. We filled our time in with sightseeing, Howard buying himself some rather nice shirts and a pair of deck shoes that were better suited for that type of weather. We agreed to eat when I got back from picking up the car. I got a taxi to the garage and got back into my own car. It felt so funny after the hire car. I made my way gingerly back to the center of the town, but it was hard at that busy time of day, and I continually got lost. I found myself near the hotel, but as there were several with a similar name, I made a wrong turn and was back out of my way. It was getting darker and darker and I was getting more and more strained by the effort. At one point I realized that I was driving without lights, not remembering when I had turned them off. I thought about stopping and ringing Howard but decided against it, even though I wanted to tell him I was running late or ask for directions, as I was in now what seemed a very dodgy area. I had to keep going and drove and drove until I eventually I found the hotel area again and my way back into the hotel room. Howard was pleased to see me. He had started to worry and tell himself crazier and crazier stories about my whereabouts. Fear and worry does such harm to us when we do not know what is going on and there are little ways of finding out, but we were all back together again, so we put Honey in the car and decided to look for somewhere to eat. The hotel did not seem the place to eat, so went back down the street where we had been in earlier. We had treated ourselves to rather fancy ice creams and now were entering a rather smart restaurant. It was set out for a large party, but they found us a table for two. We chose some lovely food to eat and had excellent wine to accompany it. I was tired and weary, but the food and ambiance of the place brought me round and I started to relax.

We had an excellent meal of turbot with asparagus and endive in a hollandaise sauce. When it came time for a sweet I chose cheese instead, and the sheep's cheese was just delicious with the red wine we were drinking. It was one of those meals you will always remember for the moments you shared, just like five days earlier sitting by the Mediterranean. The awful start to the night had ended very well indeed, and we had our car back and the dog could stay with us in the hotel. Even though it was not our sort of hotel at all, it met our needs and we were able to park not far away, which helped no end.

The next day we had breakfast in the hotel and then got back in the truck to go home. It was so good to have Howard next to me to help me find my way, and soon we were heading back to the mountains. Gradually I got used to driving at the other side of the car and to the feel to our truck as opposed to the hire car, which was so much newer. We stopped for coffee in a very attractive place and bought provisions in a supermarket on the way home. We were both tense and tired from all that had gone on over the last ten days, and it was good to get back to base; even the mountain road felt better. There was a certain freedom being away from the hustle and bustle of the modern world in this little village, and it was great to be able to let Honey out to do her own thing with the village dogs. It was so far from what we had come from in England and so far from the awful tourist hotels. I got back into Jean Houston's book, *The Hero and the Goddess,* with a certain trepidation. Was I really on that type of odyssey? I had managed the broken-down car on the mountain road. What other things had I to deal with, and would I be able to cope? I worked my way though it, , obviously not going into group work, as there was only me doing it, but I found it very interesting. Jean's book had exercises in it to help you understand the metaphors of going on such a voyage of discovery. Being safe and knowing what comes next as a routine is very reassuring, but life is not like that and I had to deal with it. Yuck. Communications eased, but the cheap phone I had bought with a Spanish sim card still did not work in that area, while the Vodaphone decided to let at least a few messages through. We slept twelve hours that night, so exhausted were we from all out adventures by the sea. The book inspired me to write poetry, and it was good to be able to create again after such a long time. We all felt more relaxed now and sauntered around the place not going out in the car and just getting back into village life. I cooked us a good tea and later watched some television. I found a program on women aviators and felt a kinship with them. They were so inspiring; I just loved them and their bravery. It made me very happy, and it was good again to have communication when we had been without it for so long. Sunday was a similar low-key day making paella for lunch and watching the world on the television. At first when we got there I could only get rubbish programs, but for some reason now I was able to see the news even though it was difficult to watch with another earthquake in Turkey and the people of Libya rising up—so much unrest in the world.

Monday was altogether different. It was a horrible day. I had all my buttons pushed at once. We went into the small town nearby, but not before I had to shout at the workmen who had come to do the road outside our house. They had left us no way to get out and were busy digging up the path with noisy machinery. I shouted to them "Attencion" several times before they stopped and let us out, and then I had to get the car down that mountain road. I took Howard to show him Suzanne and Peter's shop while I went round to try yet another café. Suzanne and Peter lived close by to us up the mountain. Again I could not get on and so had to go back to the hotel where I had to pay to go on their machine. So it meant I could only do the minimum and was not able to find us another place to stay. It rained all day and when we got back the path in front of our house was all dug up and wet and muddy and so I had to carry Honey through it all as she would be filthy. When it rained like that water dripped in through the dining room roof so I felt very miserable indeed at the fact we could not get out and inside we had the constant dripping. It brought up all my claustrophobia issues all over again and the feelings of being stuck and not able to move on that I find hard to deal with.   I suppose it could be called impatience. It all seemed a metaphor for my early life with the lack of communication and the inability to get away from the violence I witnessed as a child. For a child growing up in the period I did, parents did not talk about the issues they faced and what was going on for them so you ended up frightened and having no understanding of what was happening around you. I had to deal with it. The only way to go was inside.

It was a very hard few hours getting to the root/route of it all and trying to come to terms with it. The next day I took the day off and just relaxed with the knowledge that we had to leave this place somehow. Howard took Honey for a walk and noticed the state of the mountain above the road and too realized this was not the place for us. It was time to move on. I needed to discuss it with our hostess, but she remained evasive. I had to let it go for the time being, and anyway I was in no mood to talk. I felt particularly hopeless. All I could do was escape into the pages of the book.

The next day was just as bad. The men were there again, this time laying the concrete right in front of the house. We were trapped all day, so back to the book I went. I made the most of the time but was feeling pretty low from lack of sleep. Honey had wanted to go to the loo at three o'clock in the morning, so we went out. The streets of the village were lit, but the entire street was such a mess that you had to be extra careful where you put your feet. Wednesday was another day when we had to lie low. I hated feeling like a trapped animal, but that was what I was. I tried to make the best of it—we all did—but it was hard. It wasn't until the workmen had gone in the late afternoon that I realized that they had just left the concrete but had not left us a way out again. Honey was desperate to get out and go for a walk after spending all day in the house. I had to somehow tell her that it was impossible, but it was not easy to do with a small dog. I was in the dining room when I heard a lot of scuffling and a scream. I did not know what had happened, but I soon did when I went to the door. It turned out that Honey was not going to take "no" for an answer and on seeing Lucinda walk into her yard had jumped off the top balcony down past Lucinda into the cement. For some extraordinary reason she was not hurt but

27

just winded. Perhaps she was internally bleeding. I stared at my little dog as we all crowded round. Of course she loved the attention; she had been missing out all day. Lucinda in a way felt responsible and tried to check her out. Honey was moving perfectly fine. All limbs seemed to be intact, and she was showing no sign of shock. There was a bit of cement that will always be Honey's, as it holds the impression of her body there forever.I could not understand why she had not hurt herself, she had jumped down over thirty feet? How is it she could soon go and play and not think anything about it? There were so many questions. Howard was in shock. He had just watched his precious dog make a decision that meant she would fly through the air. He had watched her get up on the balustrade and had tried to call her down, but she had turned, looked at him, and gone for it.

We had let her down perhaps by not walking on the wet concrete and forcing our way out. The dog had no qualms— she wanted out, and that was what she did. We spent all evening discussing it and thinking it over as we tried to sleep. I wondered if she would wake up the next morning after having internal injuries we just could not see, but the next day she was playing again. I texted the woman who bred her to see if any of her siblings were as crazy as our dog and found out that she was one of a kind. She was our Honey, and she was so special.

Honey spent the next day playing and jumping and twisting in the air. It was to be our last day there. There was no way we could stay now in this pretty village with her newfound tricks. She might do it again, and the next time she may find she was not so lucky. I took lots of photos to remind me of the house and the countryside around it, and of course of the cement mark she had left. We discussed it with Lucinda and came to an agreement that was satisfactory on both sides. We decided to go further north and visit friends in Valencia. We spent time packing and saying good-bye to the mountains we had grown to love. It would be hard to leave, but we felt we had no other choice.

Chapter Two
VALENCIA

You cannot imagine the relief I felt when we finally came down the mountain for the last time. I was still a bit in shock but really glad that I had made it and I would not have to go up there again as if I were on a white-knuckle ride. Even down there the way to the village was not the easiest road to drive with its many difficult corners, but we arrived and I did a few jobs that needed to be done before we set on our way. I always find it difficult to move on; I notice the fear of the unknown but go anyway. Here we were leaving what we thought would be our home for the next six months to check out Valencia. The day started well; the weather was gorgeous. We had been down to the main road several times now because of the car, so that bit was straightforward. We even started to get to a place of lightness and gaiety as we got on the main road around Spain. I was well used to driving on the right-hand side of the road now and liked the Spanish road system. It was easy to understand. I had heard two women talking before I set off about how hard it was to drive in Spain. I was thankful that I had not taken it on board, as I was having a totally different experience and probably would not have attempted it at all if I had scared myself by their words.

I drove past Almeria and the area where we had stayed some weeks before. In fact we ended up stopping at the same garage for petrol. Soon after we found ourselves in new territory, so it became an adventure all over again. I just kept heading north. Eventually we left the main road looking for somewhere for lunch. One restaurant looked very nice from outside, but the food left a lot to be desired. Howard had chicken soup that seemed to be a stock cube with one tiny piece of chicken in it. I love globe artichokes and so had a salad of them. The whole plate was full of them. It swam in them. I do like them, but to be presented with so many was rather offputting. I am not sure I have eaten any since then! With all the upset of the last few nights I was soon getting tired and so started looking somewhere for sleep. We could see the sea and what looked a pretty coastline from our road, but how to get onto the lower road? We tried.

I drove round and round. We were now in the home of the Costas; well, the home of the many English who flock to Spain for sea, sand, and tans. It was not the sort of lifestyle we go for and so felt that it was not the place to be in for long. Unfortunately life does not always work out the way you think it should. After many a wrong turn and lack of information to find a more suitable spot for the night we were forced to drive into an underground car park and leave the dog there while we asked around for a hotel that would put us up for the night. The dog hated the car park, but we had not much choice about it, as I was now too tired to drive anymore and that might have been dangerous given the road conditions. After a wait we were told that there was a room and that they had WIFI, which was going to be a help. We could eat in the hotel too. To us it was a place of nightmares; to others it would be a dream come true. The town was full

31

of hotels, and to us it was ugly. We did not fit in at all with the other clientele, but as we could get Honey out for walks around the area in the rain it was better than nothing, and perhaps I would get some sleep too. When we went out in the rain with her, it was quite slippery underfoot with all the marble in the pavements, so I took it nice and gently so I did not land on the hard ground.

I do not think I have ever eaten such awful food. It was complete and utter trash. It was another help-yourself arrangement with some meals being served, but we hardly ate anything because it was so awful. The soup was similar to what Howard had earlier; it was supposed to be cream of asparagus soup, but there was no taste at all. However, we did get some sleep and Honey was okay in the car. That was the main thing, breakfast being as tasteless as the dinner the night before. I think they must have watered down the juices, because I could not even drink them. Yet our priorities had been met. We all got back into the car and drove north again. I had gotten hold of my other friend on Skype, and we arranged to go to meet her that day.

It was just after that when we found ourselves in unknown territory, and then the rain really started to come down. It was as if the sky had been cut in half and all the water that had accumulated in the clouds had been let loose all at one time. I could hardly see where I was going. I got into the inner lane, as some people must have had far better windshield wipers than me or more confidence in their ability to go fast in all weather. I might drive reasonably well, but I do not take those sorts of risks. It would ease off for a while and then pour again. I ended up stopping at a gas station to get a coffee. I took it back to the car and got some sweets. I had driven quite a way, and it was good to stop. The whole forecourt was like a small sea, and there were only drivers who had taken themselves off the road to rest and recuperate. Surely it would let up soon. We spent a while there, but finally I felt that it was time to restart the journey. My friend Liz lived not far away, but rather than try to find her in the rain with little information about where she lived we decided to wait till another day to venture to her part of the world.

The rain eased off a bit and we went towards Mary's house; well, the meeting spot. This time we did not stop at all for lunch but went straight there. First there were a few false turns, should I say mistakes, and then we were back on the road again. We were to meet at the local garage, but because of the rain and not stopping in on Liz we were early and so went to a bar for a drink and let her know we were near. Some time previously she had invited us to her house, and a few other people I knew had stayed, but basically I was not sure what to expect. She did not seem to get on with her husband and perhaps blamed him for the stalemate in their relationship. Yet I still felt that it was the right place to go and went with an open mind. She was shopping with her daughter when I sent her a text but said she would be there shortly and asked if I would get some bread from the supermarket across the road. I did not mind, of course. Where we had lived before in Spain the shops were closed quite early on the weekend, so it was good to see how other parts of Spain got on. Here things seemed a lot easier, but then it was not fiesta time and bank holiday rolled into one. Maybe our timing was better?

It was good to see her. I had not seen her for about a year and a half, and she had lost a lot of weight on some strange meat diet. I am not sure she looked a lot better, because at our age losing weight can be a difficult remodeling effect. Lines and skin can take on new postures that do not always work, but if you feel better about yourself and healthier, then it is the way to go. The main thing is that she was enthusiastic to see us and our little dog and soon we were following her and her daughter and her grandson to her home.

The thing for us was the mountain road. After the one we had come down two days earlier this seemed a total doddle. Bumpy in places, it would have put a lot of people off, but in our four-by-four with my newly acquired experience at these sorts of roads I was happy to drive down this one. There was no sheer drop at either side, and there were trees and it was wider too. You just had to be careful around potholes and strange mounds, but as I said it was just so simple after our earlier experience.

My friend's husband was in one of his strange moods when we got there, and I had to check inside to see if we had done the right thing. I ignored his moods, and we had some lunch and then went for a delightful walk in the area around them. It was very beautiful. I should have changed my shoes into a more solid pair, as the paths were wet and muddy and the pair I had on soon took on an orange tone from the mud. I saw a huge frog on our walk, which made me happy. Luckily I still have the child's joy of nature and can appreciate it in all its wonder.

We had been given her daughter's room and so dragged a few things in from the car. We had no idea how long we were staying, but as Halloween was fast approaching we were expected to stay for the party that was going to take place to celebrate the time of year. It was odd to be in the house, but it was good to be around people of all generations and chat on so many subjects and to catch up with my friend.

The next day, Sunday, we ended up getting ready for the party by making lanterns and later went to a local bar for dinner. It was good fun and enjoyable trying out all the new foods chosen by her daughter, who was well used to the Spanish way of life by then and was working as a translator as she could now speak the language so well.

The next day I took the car into the nearest town with my friend and her grandson in tow. It was a twisty road but again not as bad as before. I was in a bit of shock as it happened, as that morning we had been chatting and I had mentioned one man I had met and she asked me how this had happened. Some years ago my friend had lent me his book and I had thoroughly enjoyed it. Some months previously I had attended a talk given by him. A second time I had been in his presence and was telling her about it when she asked me how I got involved. I told her another man's name and she gasped. I had been on a committee with him, and as it turned out, this man was the reason her second marriage had collapsed. She had lost touch with him, but he obviously had meant a lot through the breakup of that marriage; she was now on her third marriage. This was all completely new to me. So there we were all those years later discussing someone I had ended up giving advice to about his current relationship. Again it showed how we seem to be going one way and there in the background is another story altogether.

How can you take anything for granted? These people with many faces, one presented to the world but another hidden from view if they can possibly help it—do they do it on purpose or is it something they cannot help?

The other shock was that she had offered to rent me their flat for three hundred euros a month so we could have somewhere to stay and continue our time in Spain. She wanted me to stay for six months so we could be there over Christmas and have time to look at houses in the area if we wanted to live there. She was full of enthusiasm for the idea and doing a great selling job on it. We had only expected to be there for a few days, but six months? I needed to discuss it with Howard.

It was Samhain, or The day of the Dead, or Halloween , and the party was put off to the bank holiday, which was the next day, All Saints Day. So the lanterns had to wait.

Honey seemed to enjoy her new home and had got round my friend's husband and was allowed to sit on the furniture while his own dog was scooted off most of the time. I made salads for the party and went to collect Mary's daughter and her boyfriend from down the road. He had a car, but it was not one he wanted damaged on the rocky road up to the house, so he left it where the road was kinder and we would pick them up from there. Unfortunately, because of the bank holiday people and cars were all over the track, and instead of going down the mountain road I ended going up and up till I was very clear I had gone wrong. Somehow I found my way back to the house and left that job to her husband.

I had a friend who died the year before, and that day was his birthday—or would have been. I wore the jewelry he had given me to celebrate his life. He had been a kind man and we had had a good friendship and he had introduced me to a lot of new things. It was strange not to be able to talk to him anymore. A girlfriend had had a birthday the day before, her sixtieth, and I had texted her on the day. I had missed her fiftieth too, as I had been in Wales then; how those years had just drifted away to leave us with memories. Luckily I spend most of my time in the moment now, which makes life so much better with little thought of what there might have been if only.

The party was a success, I think, even with the few people who turned up. We sat on the veranda and had lots to eat and drink. The main success for me was the cheesecake the daughter's boyfriend's mother made. Unfortunately because so few turned up there was a lot of bits left over and something never cooked, but we had celebrated well. Later in the evening another friend turned up with his mother. I noticed from her body language that she was fascinated with me but never found out why. She was a very pleasant woman, and we got on well. When they had gone we went to bed, but by then the lights had gone out, as their life was powered by an electric generator and it did not work properly. So we lit the room with candles, which are lovely but difficult when there were so many rooms to light and steps to fall down.

After a while we decided to take up the offer of the flat downstairs. It would help us stabilize for a while and give us chance to look around another area of Spain. The only problem we found was that because of their relationship they did not have the greatest energies around them, as they always seemed to be bickering, and I hoped it would not drag us down too much. The flat was better than being in one bedroom, so we paid them some money and took all our possessions down there. In the end we did not have the entire flat but the front part, as they had too many possessions of their own to move out. It was not so bad for a short-term base. I could not see us staying there all that long even though my friend was trying to get us to stay for six months. She was a nervous wreck and would come down to check things out and ask us numerous questions. At one point she removed all the silver and took it upstairs just in case we decided to run away with it! We were often interrupted like that. What could have been relaxing was becoming quite difficult with all her needs, and

then we were told we could not download too much from
the Internet, as it ran out. I had never heard anything like
it before and tried to understand what she was saying. Two
nights before she had been doing that all evening when she
was singing with music that had been downloaded and I never
noticed any change in power that was coming through, if that
is how her type of Internet worked. I started to feel that we
were being put under stress by her constant need to control
us. Nevertheless we tried to make the most of our new home
away from home underneath their own place. I added a few
of my own things here and there to give a little more of the
feeling we had a place to call our own for the time being.
The thing about us being there at Christmas was being pushed
basically because she wanted us to look after our home for her
when they went away. I pointed out that we would then be
house sitting, which would take us to another arrangement
altogether. I talked about going to France for that period, but
she said it would be difficult to get over the mountains and
would be better there and would not cost us anything for that
period and Howard's mother would be welcome too. The
pressure went on with a list of houses that were for sale in the
area. As much as she has been a friend for a long time this type
of behavior did not seem friendly at all. She was becoming a
salesperson hoping for a good commission if we bought one
of the properties. I kept pointing out that we had only just
arrived and it was far too soon to decide whether this was the
place where we should set up home.

It was all very difficult, but she would be going to England
shortly, leaving us with the husband. It was all such a shame,
and I understood that her life was not easy, trying to make
ends meet in the new country they called home and keeping
the house up to standard so they could make money from

visitors during the summer months. They had obviously spent a lot of money on some of the areas, with very attractive bathrooms and kitchens. The views were lovely, and they had a pool that had to be maintained too. Honey had Piglet to play with. The other dogs I was not sure about, as they were locked in a compound, and there were several cats around that were very interesting. In the village where we had come from Honey was just getting used to her freedom and being able to wander about with the street dogs, especially Frodo, who just liked to play. Now there was Piglet and long walks to go on where there was little traffic and few people to jump up and down on. We would set off past the houses and walk along the high banks with the river gurgling in the bottom. It was ferocious when we got there from all the rains but soon settled down again. It was glorious and was a very beautiful area. I loved setting off with my lovely dog staring into the distant and enjoying the beauty that was around me. It was the first time I had come across the oak holly and the carob tree. It was also good to see many flowers still in bloom so late in the year. Once we got down the path I checked to see if it was okay to let Honey off the lead and just let her go. It was a wonderful sight to see our small dog racing and moving with such grace and speed; she loves to run, as do I, if I remembered to put my running shoes on we could both have a go. Another thing that I so enjoyed about this time of year in Spain was that it was still okay to wear light clothes, clothes that would be put away by now in England, ready for the next May. Here I was still wearing them and letting my skin brown in the warm air.

Another funny thing happened when I moved downstairs into the flat—my brown leather flip-flops disappeared, and to this day I have not gotten them back. I mentioned that they were not there, but there was no explanation as to where they had gone. I know they came with me, as they were my favorite shoes to wear in the warm climate, and I am not quite so gone not to know I had them in the house at some time. It seems they are to be one of the mysteries of the universe, just like the Bermuda Triangle.

Another lovely part of our life there for Honey was one that of the cats allowed himself to be played with. He was called Zorro, and after a few days they would hang around together. It was such a joy to see the two together—sometimes they would even sleep together. Zorro's brother got pushed out by the two of them together as he was not as friendly and would try to bat Honey rather than be gentle even though Honey would have liked to be friends. He was not sure about our dog.

One Saturday we went to the market in one of the close towns. I took my friend and her grandson to pick up her daughter so they could go round the market. I was not struck by the market at all, as it was full of cheap things—what I mean about being cheap is I thought the quality was not good. My friend bought a jumper and a handbag and gifts for her grandson, leaving her with no money for food. Somehow I had become a taxi, or so it felt. I do not mind helping people, but I do not like, as is true of most people, being used. There seemed very little give and take in all of this, especially when I was asked to hurry in the supermarket, as I was needed to buy her food and she was waiting for me at the checkout. My friend wanted to stay longer, but I was tired because of lack of sleep again. The night before Howard and I had been irritated and had our first row. Somehow it seemed as if the energy around us had seeped in and we were becoming like our hosts. Luckily we had gotten over it and gone back to our true selves, leaving us shaken by the incident. I did not want to be away for too long in this strange tension and wanted to get back to my husband.

Our evening together went well, so at least I slept well again and felt better for it. We had a quiet Sunday and just mooched about the place, taking photos of Honey and Zorro, who were constantly together. On Monday my friend brought up the Christmas thing again, but it was all too soon for me. My husband and I were both not sure we wanted the responsibility of looking after somebody's place and their animals when communications were not so good in the area. The whole trip was about us looking at other options for places to live, and if we stayed there we would not have the freedom to do that. Hence I tried to slow the pace down again.

At least I had started writing again, some poetry at our first home in Spain and now some larger pieces. It felt good to be able to do this, as I do enjoy the art of writing whatever the outcome. One evening as two couples we sat and talked and I realized that I was standing up for myself with her husband. He was being very sarcastic about the people I knew. I was aware that I was not doing it out of ego; it was just a matter of fact and so did not need to feel bad about what I said. It showed me just how much I had grown over the last few years and how I could be compassionate and understanding with a man whom I had found it quite hard to get on with in the past. I certainly would have gotten upset by his attitude then, but was not allowing myself that upset now. Perhaps that was why we all needed this experience?

We had only a few days left together before my friend went to work in London, so she celebrated with authentic paella made by a friend of hers. We had a pleasant afternoon chatting and laughing together even though the weather was not so good and watched a DVD at night called *The Secret Life of Bees*. I had seen it before but she had not, and we had both read and enjoyed the book. I love bees, as I do most creatures, even though I am now allergic to their sting, yet cannot stop the fascination with them and their lives. It is a lovely film and shows the injustice of prejudice and the sadness that invades our lives and our need to not let it get too upsetting. The reality of course is that we need to feel; if we don't then we are not really here at all. I went to bed sensing more joy around the place, a lot better about things.

The weather was better the next day, and I went out with her family to check out the outlying area. Her husband drove, so I was able to sit back and look around me. I really enjoyed myself, especially with her grandson. I drew him out of himself, and it was good to see a smile on his face rather than experience the sulky boy he often portrayed.

On her last day the water heater finally gave up, making it even harder to do things. It meant having to go up into the house and take all our wash cloths etc to the back bathroom if we wanted a hot shower in the morning. My friend's husband tried to mend it, but it did not work. We also started to smell gassy smells, but I was talked down and was given the idea that I was imagining them. It was a weird day altogether as we waited for her to leave. We had come back from the town early, as she said she was going at two and we wanted to say "good-bye" to her, but in fact she did not leave till six, and they all were in a bad mood then. So what could have been a gentle start to her journey ended up being a drama all over again. Our relationship now seemed flawed by our time there. She had been under enormous pressure from family members, which may have accounted for some of her behavior. I suppose

I had changed a lot over the years, too, but even though we had been together some time there was never really any true connection. Even though she said we were like sisters, I could not feel any real affection from her. Had her old flame ignited something I did not understand?

We left the flat on Thursday to look for my other friend, Liz, who lived about half an hour away. It was an easy journey to her place on yet another gorgeous day. We found the town she lived in far more easily than we had expected but had no idea at all where to go. The address we had been given seemed a little vague, but nevertheless we were going to check it out and see if we could find her. We stopped on the edge of the town for a walk around and found a café where there were what seemed to be two English couples. The first one was not sure what I wanted, but the second couple was able to tell me exactly where we had to go and were very helpful. We needed to be in the center of the town by the sea. The town center seemed very attractive. It took a little while to find a parking spot, but we were lucky enough to find a car park and leave our car there.

Back at the main square I found an estate agent and so walked in to see if they could help. The agent in fact was English, which of course helped enormously. I suppose most of their trade was from English people buying Spanish apartments. He pointed me across the road to the block of flats there. The one he pointed at looked as if it was being done up, but I went across all the same. I looked to see if there were any names that would point out that she lived there but could not see anything that made sense. We wandered around the block looking at all the numbers; the one place that would have made sense was not there. Then I spied a post person at the other side of the road. I went to ask her, but she pointed me in another direction altogether. This happened again when I went into the English second-hand shop that was on the corner. Trying to follow their advice I could not see anything at all that fitted. Howard sat down while I continued my search, but to no avail, I walked round and round peering at numbers and names, hunting desperately and hoping to see my friend's name. It was now lunchtime, so we walked to the sea and found a café where we could eat and drink. We sat in the sun and stared at the blue sea and wonderful clear sky. I decided to give up the search for the day and just have a walk along the front. The whole place seemed geared up for the English, with cafés all down the front and some quite pleasant shops. I kept hoping to bump into my friend and tried to imagine what she would look like after about ten years. She had said she was not well and had given up driving, so I added a few extra years on for that. We had lost touch when I was living in Wales and she moved to Spain, but then I had gotten her English address and she had written back and said it was nice to have a pen-friend. I had hoped we would be able to carry on where things had parted, but it seemed it was not going to happen. I bought a few things at the local supermarket and we made our way back to the flat. As it was so easy to find we decided that we would come back another day and resume the search. Maybe things would make sense that time; I hoped so.

Our lives took on a more serene pace with only the husband at home. We spent more time together and enjoyed those moments sharing joy and the beauty around us. On November 11, 2011, we drove into town for some supplies and I noticed that it was 11:11 exactly, perfect timing on such a day. As I write this it says I am on page eleven of eleven, so again it is all working perfectly, as some would say. We had gotten into having coffee in the street cafés and just taking in the views and the ambience of Spain. I love to people-watch, and they were just the right places to be to do it. It was such a world away from the life we were used to and having time out among people.

We were waiting for the post to come from England. Even though there were some beautiful areas there, we were not really happy in the flat. The generator was always going off, leaving us in the dark in more ways than one. Luckily we were very good at making the most of a situation, but it was still hard with night lights the only means of light when it was quite early in the evening. It was far too soon to go to sleep, and so we muddled on. We often went to town to check if the post had arrived. In the meantime I experimented with Spanish cookery and made us delicious meals with the ingredients I bought. I loved the challenge of this.

I had taken up my friend, Roshi Joan Halifax's book *The Fruitful Darkness* and read the chapter *The Way of the Mountain*. I had picked the "Changing Woman" from my Goddess book as inspiration and marveled that Joan mentioned the Changing Woman in her passage on the mountain. I also dreamed of Lulu for some reason and remembered seeing her with her first husband, Maurice Gibb, when I was on Kensington High Street. I also bumped into Gerry Rafferty there. It turns out that both men were alcoholics. Was my drawing power to this disease so strong that I pulled both toward me? Or was it just again pure coincidence? I then read the words Baker Street in the other book I was reading, "Baker Street" being Gerry Rafferty's big hit. More strange coincidences; I have so many and so many through books I am reading.

I marveled at the synchronicity in it all and yet felt disappointed at the same time. The flat was miserable and the colors are dull. Thank goodness for the view outside the window. I wanted to get out but needed to be patient. We needed to get our mail so we could tie things up back in England and sort out bits that we were unable to do before we left. Joan's chapter on the mountain was helpful and hopeful, and I was glad I took the time to reread it. It was one of those books you could pick up from time to time for inspiration, by another remarkable woman whom I had met on my many journeys. She certainly inspires many other women.

Barcelona had always been a place I wanted to see, and with my birthday coming up I wondered which was the best way to get myself there. Howard was not that interested in going and had wanted to take me in one of his romantic moments. In the real light of day, and having the small dog, it seemed quite a difficult thing to do. We had planned to leave Honey with the grandson but then realized that we just could not leave her. I looked on the Internet for ideas and planned to stay at a place outside Barcelona so I could take a train in on my own and explore that part of Spain. We have gotten into our head that France was a better option and the place to be for Christmas. We do not want the noisy generator and the smells that seemed to be coming from it, the sea of carbon monoxide that rose to the flat. The walks were my salvation; I pick wild rosemary on one of them and took it home to flavor a lamb dish I was making. We heard our host, Mary's husband, screaming at his neighbor, and we shuddered. What sadness does that man carry and what anger?

I wrote this poem:

> The mountain stands before me,
> Solid, unquestioning
> I hear it calling from

Time to time
It seems to know my name.
I am Changing Woman
Deep in my bones
I know her to be me
We walk up the mountain together
Holding hands
We kneel to its greatness
Humbled but happy
At our part in it
It in us
Then we skip down
Free, freer, Free.

Howard had to go back to England, so I decided to book myself into the place near Barcelona I had found. At least there, alone with the dog, I would feel better. I had gotten to like my friend's husband, but the sadness of the place would be too much for me on my own. Howard and I enjoyed each other and our talks; I would not have that when he was away from me. I needed to be in a place that felt right and felt safe. This did not do the trick. I got back to the woman on the internet who had the place near Barcelona and confirm a week's stay so at least we would be somewhere else for my birthday.

As the days went by I noticed more and more the smells around the place. I did not know whether it was because when I came back from one of our lovely walks in the fresh air the smell of the generator or the water system seemed just far worse. I started to sleep badly and got depressed because of the situation. The waiting for something to get better and feel right was only days, but it seemed a lot longer. My husband

and I both ended up being tense; getting out of there to the nearest village was my escape. I went down for post and food and wandered around the market. It felt so much better not being around the house and the strange smells. As I walked back to the car I spied a red rose on the ground and felt that it had been dropped for me. I always do that with flowers that are being left in strange places, and so home it came and straight into water so I could at least see some beauty in this odd situation. The cats kept coming in as soon as we opened the door, and the small dog too. There was no end to the intrusions. If you left the window open to get in some air you either got the cats in or more noise and fumes from the generator. I curled up into a ball when I could not take any more. I realized later that it was the right thing to have done, a sense of holding myself safe. I just wanted release; we both did. The next day we took ourselves out again, this time to Gandia, and had a lovely day in the sun. It was very warm, and we found a delightful street with lots of going on to have a coffee and watch the world go by and forget our troubles. I bought myself some nice cord trousers, which cheered me up. We both felt a lot better for getting out and about and wandered around looking at the original home of the Borgias and explored back streets and the main area in the center of the town. Going back to the car was another thing, as it took a little while to locate where we had parked it in an underground car park, but we did get there in the end and back to the place where we were living. I was pleased to be able to get on the Internet and read about those who were trying to change the system in New York. It seemed so positive to me. Apparently the authorities had set the guards on the occupy movement and when they were rushed what was left was a book by Aldous Huxley. On reading his ideas again I realized that those ideas had been mine for a long time and it was no wonder Huxley had been an early hero of mine. I was glad something was being done at last about the greed and corruption in the world and sent money to support the cause. Is change inevitable? Who knows—it certainly seems to be, and for us it changed very quickly.

I started to feel worse and spent the next day in bed, my body feeling awful and with it a lack of energy. Mary's husband came down, and we told him about the smells—well, you could hardly miss them. It was decided that the fridge was the culprit. The ice cream had melted and a new gas canister had been applied. For some reason it was not turned off. To keep the cats out we had to put mesh at the windows, and as I lay in bed I could hear them trying to remove it so they could get in. In the end we had to close the windows at the front and leave the bathroom window open. It probably saved our life, because the next morning we both were in a lot of pain. All our glands ached, and we felt sick through and through. At one point I know I had been giving up and did not care if I lived or died—perhaps in some ways death had been a way out—but by four in the morning I knew I had to crawl out of the place on my hands and knees if necessary. There were times when I felt I could not breathe at all. I obviously could, but it left me feeling even more scared and worried about our situation. I got up and forced myself out and starting packing bags and suitcases; nothing now mattered but leaving. I was like a tornado even though I felt dreadful; this seemed like a case of survival at all costs. Now I wanted to survive, and it meant leaving. We went down for breakfast and post, and luckily the envelope we were waiting for was there. We had hoped to be spending the day looking for my friend Liz again. Now that was out of the question, and so we drove back to the flat. Luckily the dogs had been taken out for a walk and the gates were open so we could drive right down to the back of the flat and load our belongings. The husband was now staring at us from the balcony and wondered what was up. We told him what had happened. He was now shocked and upset at our plight and offered us money back on the flat. It was his birthday the next day, so Howard told him to keep the money as a birthday present. I do not know how I managed it all, but somehow I was able to drive the car back down the track to drop rubbish off at the bins before we drove away. It was not the last time, because we realized that my husband's long-distance glasses were back at the flat. I drove there yet again to find that they had been behind a curtain so there was no way we could have seen them when we were packing. I left a birthday card and the rose on the table for our host. He had tried to help the best he could. We just wanted to get away and try to get fresh air into our lungs. I was glad to be alive and heading away. Death had stared me in the face yet again on this tour, and I had gotten through this test even though my chest and lungs had been affected and nothing would be the same again.

Chapter Three
CATALONIA

I do not know how we managed to get anywhere that day, especially with the lack of sleep I had and the amount of fumes we had taken in during the night. After all the driving to and from the house we finally got off and drove as far as we could. We headed for Castello and felt that it would be a safe place to stay. I did wonder if we should go to a hospital for a checkup but then decided against it. We just wanted to get away. We stopped at a service station for something to eat, but the food tasted awful. We had the taste of the gas in our mouths, or that is what it felt like. I ended up leaving it, which says something for my state, as I hate leaving food and hate waste—I had to be in a bad way. We eventually got to the town, but with our late start to the day it was hard to get parked. We did find a hotel but could not get near it to park. We stopped some way off but could not find our way back to it. We were in a bit of a state and consequently had gotten a parking ticket by the time we got back to the car. I did not see it until I had set off and did not know how to deal with it at all, not surprising really. I just started driving round the town looking for something that said stop and stay here but did not see anything and ended up going toward the port. Hotels seemed completely absent from view as we drove round and round. I stopped to ask in the end and got pointed along the front. We found one hotel, and I walked across the road to ask if they had any rooms. The man behind the desk seemed to have no idea, so after looking around and not being particularly happy with what I saw, I got back in the car and carried on with my search. We eventually found a hotel right near the docks. It was able to provide WIFI and looked clean and well run. I felt better about this place even if Honey would have to stay in the car for the night. The area was well lit, and in fact we could see the car from the balcony overlooking the street. I showered to wake myself up and feel a little better. Some of the symptoms were subsiding, and just the fact we were away from the place was an enormous relief. The hotel did not provide an evening meal, but just across the road was a line of seafood restaurants. After taking Honey for a walk and giving her some food we went to get something for ourselves. I noticed as we walked along the sound of birds but could not see them as I looked up into the trees above me. The meal was good, and as Howard had steak Honey got some of that too. I got a healthy salad, or so I hoped. We both carried an enormous relief that we were alive and that we had gotten through the ordeal. Other worries seemed small, and life took on a different sheen. We were away and free and had other days to play with and of course slept well.

The next morning I went to the balcony to look out at the world and at our car down the road. What I realized was that the noise the night before had been of starlings roosting in the trees. Our balcony was directly opposite the birds. What joy I experienced as I watched these remarkable creatures leave the trees in hundreds and do their remarkable display. It was such a gift to start the day, so different from the day before. How can you equate the two?

Honey got a good walk to start the day. We wandered around the docks, and there were plenty of cats for her to want to chase. It was so good to be there in that interesting district. I had rung the woman whom we hoped to stay with next to see if we could come early because of what happened. She said "yes," so we had a place for the next ten days. We went into a very good continental breakfast with fruit, so even that helped us get to our next port of call. Ever optimistic, we went back to the main highway and found gas just in time. It all seemed remarkably easy after all the hardship we had encountered earlier on, but we were not going to complain when we were just glad to be alive.

Catalonia here we come.

It was a much better journey than the day before, but of course it was—we were feeling a whole lot better and the strain of the last few weeks had left us. I contacted our new host. She was shopping for our tea and told us to go straight there. The place was open and we could make ourselves at home. It was a lovely day, and at first we missed the turning. We rang her again and she explained the easiest way to get there. It was easy except that we counted the masais, farmhouses belonging to vineyards, wrongly and ended up at one up a hill. The woman I asked was very helpful, and we were soon at our next place to stay. I had stopped at the village bakery and bought some very nice looking pieces of pizza. They were something I do not normally go for, but these looked really delicious so I succumbed to temptation. For the third time on our trip to Spain we unloaded all our possessions into our new home and looked around ourselves. This time we were in what had been the donkey shed on what they call a masai surrounded by grape fields. The views were again lovely. As we did not know how near the next shops were and when they opened and what places there were to eat in the area we had arranged for our host to cook us a meal that evening and have breakfast supplied the next day. So really there was nothing to do but wait for her return and make ourselves at home. I had brought with me some little bits and pieces to add to the house, the main one being a yellow dragonfly that sticks to the windows. I put it on the door to the balcony, and again it looked just right, as if it had been there all the time. The balcony was set up with a table and chairs so you could just sit and stare at the surrounding countryside. The rest of the place was old and quite interesting, but it was not what you called comfortable for sitting for a long time. It was more set up for summer when you moved around more and spent most of the time outside. Of course most of the houses in Spain had been like that, the first house being the best set up with lovely pictures and pottery. In this place there were paintings that all had price tags on so you could buy them if you so wished. There were two large cat pictures that were quite good but not exceptional enough for me to even think about purchasing. She had a set of rules to and prices for everything that you might need. There was a whole rack of wine to buy, but she had provided us a bottle of Champagne as a moving-in present. We decided not to drink it straight away but to wait till the Friday when Howard had come back from England and drink it as a celebration of that. We went for a walk around the grape fields. It was a splendid area with lovely weather. It felt so much better than where we had been with lots of space around us rather than looking onto mountains. The evening meal was a success, and the hostess brought us a carafe of wine. I was glad I had made the decision to look after myself better and not to try to do everything and after what we had been through just to let me be spoiled for a change.

We slept reasonably well in our new home. I found myself waking early and taking Honey out for another walk among the vines. It had been wet that night and the ground was boggy, so my simple sandals were covered in the red soil of the area. I left them outside to dry off.

Lucky for us the supermarket in the nearest village was open on Sunday morning, so we took ourselves into the village to buy provisions. Yet again this journey into the village was a lot easier than the first two, and even though the road was not very wide in places it was preferable to the mountain road and the very bumpy road our last home in Spain had been on. I felt more at ease in every way here and glad we had chosen it as a place to stay when Howard was in England. That afternoon we did more exploring and went for a lovely walk, falling in love with the area and an abandoned chateau with an amazing gate. It fascinated us, and we wandered about wondering who had lived there and what secrets it held. I did not have a camera with me that day but decided I would have to come back another day and take photos of the magnificent place. I did that the next day after we had visited Villafranca to go to the post office so we could post the agreement for our holiday home in France. I did not know at the time that there was a post office in our nearest village, but it did help to go in there because it convinced me not to take the car in when I went to Barcelona the next day but to get a taxi. I took Honey out for her afternoon walk and took the photos of the lovely chateau. While we had been in the house we heard an awful argument between our hostess and some of her workers. I tried not to get too upset, but whatever happened we never saw the workers again. It sounded as if they were going to come to blows any second, but as we could not understand what was being said at this heated moment we kept well away from it all. Anyhow it was nothing to do with us.

The next day I went to Barcelona on my own. It had been one of those places I always wanted to go to and had nearly come to the conclusion that it was never going to happen in this lifetime. Yet here I was so close and I had to go and see Gaudi's work. The taxi driver came as requested and took me to the station. There I had to work out how get the right train ticket and find the correct platform for Barcelona. There were no hiccups and all went well, and soon I was sitting on the train staring at the Spanish countryside. A lot of the rivers were dry, but the further I went north the more the water started to flow. It did not take that long before I was in the center of Barcelona. Where to go now? Luckily there was a tourist office, and a guide there gave me a map to show me the way to the Gaudi shopping center. That was not quite what I had come for, so next thing I was on the underground or metro moving under the city. I managed to ask someone on the metro how to get to the famous architecture and they were very helpful, so I was able to get there and come out into the open air to see the amazing cathedral right in front of me. It was a dream come true, so out came the camera and I tried to capture its magnificence that way. Hard to do, but I got a few good photos all the same. I paid to go inside and wandered with my head held at an angle staring up at the ceilings and the lights and the windows, making myself faint from the odd position I held my neck. I could not stay in there long, preferring the outside to the inside. To me the Grand Canyon had been more awe inspiring than this manmade thing, but it was certainly fascinating and I was glad I had made the effort to check it out.

I wandered around the area looking for a coffee shop and interesting shops, but the day was grey and nothing looked particularly interesting. I did eventually find a café to have some coffee and a cheese baguette that was very good, but I had expected to find something more interesting than that in the area. Shamefully there was a McDonald's close by the cathedral, which just shows how things get muddled in so many ways. At least the fainthearted get to eat what they know. I prefer to taste the food of the region rather than a mass-marketed product that is hardly like food but some other commodity from our globalized world. I thought I had better check out another area seeing that I had made the trip and got back into the metro system and came out in another rather smart area of town that I inspected bit by bit. Nothing really tempted me, so I tried what looked like an up-market cake shop and expected to have my taste buds truly excited. Yet again outer appearance is not an indication of anything, and I was disappointed at the tasteless coffee and the rather insipid sweet. I gave up my expedition and went back to try to find the station. On the metro like in London it shows all the stops and where they lead. I thought I had read it properly and landed up at a station but could not find the railway station, so back to the metro and on to the next stop and back out again to find that I was at the right stop originally. I must have walked miles underground and on top and found myself in the station trying now to find the platform I had to leave from. I could not find the right people to ask, and some people selling tickets for trains were not very helpful, sending me to yet another queue that did not have the answer to my request. Eventually I did find a bureau that held the answer to my needs and I was given a train timetable and pointed to the right platform. No wrong train was stepped upon, and I arrived back at Villafranca in one piece. Leaving the taxi in the morning I had arranged for the taxi driver to come for me about five o'clock. I was far too early and so used the opportunity to look for a print shop so I could run off the plane ticket for Howard for the next day. I had looked earlier in the day, but now that I had been and done what I needed to do I found it easily at the other side of the road from the station. I got onto the Internet and printed the documents, and when I left the shop was told there was no charge. The taxi driver had arranged for me to meet him at the other side of the station, and so I walked over. I had chosen to do it that way because he at least knew me now and knew where I had to go. He was late, and I wondered if he was coming. But he did turn up and took me back to the place that I had left that morning. I was glad that I had taken the journey but could not see myself going back into the large town. I preferred being out in the countryside with the big blue sky above me and back with my husband and little dog. As usual, Honey greeted me as if I had been away months rather than a few hours. We were a unit again.

The next day she was going to have a completely different experience, because for the first time Howard was going away for several days. He had to go back to England and was flying from Barcelona to Newcastle. We got the same taxi driver to take him, as Howard said he would have worried too much about us getting back okay and this way he was guaranteed, he hoped, to get to the airport in time. This was one of the reasons I felt happier being in this place than the other, as it felt a lot easier to get around and safer for me to be there on my own. It would also be the first time we had been apart since we were married in April, so it was an odd experience all round.

The taxi driver was on time, so off he went. I washed some clothes and let them dry in the sun before I got into the car with Honey and went on a trip up the mountains. It seems odd to drive up the mountains when in some ways we had been glad to get away from them, but the place I saw on the sign had the same name as a book I had bought for my sixtieth birthday, so I felt I wanted to check it out. The drive was beautiful and the road very good, so I did not feel at risk as I did in the south of Spain. The sun was out and was drifting through the trees, lighting our way round the bends. I felt at ease as I drove and enjoyed the beauty around me, viewing the trees at each side of the road. We eventually got to our destination, but I could not see anything to keep me there so returned back in the direction I had come from. I went into the little town nearby and bought some bits and pieces, leaving Honey when I did my shopping in the supermarket but later taking her around with me and having a coffee at a table in the sun. Together we watched the world go by. Howard made it safely to England but was shocked at how cold it was. He would be back on the Friday, so I had another day to keep myself occupied. Honey behaved wonderfully and was a good companion. We wandered as usual later, walking through the fields of vines, and noticed how friendly the people in the area were, waving as they drove by. We had soon become part of the scenery, a woman and her little dog happily enjoying the countryside. Such a privilege after the horrible road we had to make our way down in England running down the side of the garden. There the traffic zoomed by and you hardly ever saw a friendly face; they were all too busy getting from one area to another, and the noise they made was immense compared to the vehicles here.

I was also reading an excellent book that I had found on the shelf in the kitchen/dining room. It was called *In my Father's Eyes* by Alice Walker. I loved the book, and strangely enough it mentioned *The Changing Woman*. Was I drawn to this place because of this book? Was it telling me that I, too, was a changing woman? How extraordinary to see the mention of the Changing Woman three times in such a short time. I dived into the pages and soaked up her words. I sat on the veranda and watched the sun go down with Honey by my side.

The next day we went on another little trip, this time to the village in the other direction. We had been to it when we first got there but only turned round when we realized at the other side that we had gone too far and missed the turning. I parked the car and took Honey with me to explore the place. I went around the back off the main road and found some lovely buildings to look at. It was another lovely warm day, and so it was a joy just to stroll about looking at the beauty of it all. I had a coffee sitting outside the café, letting them know that I had a dog and explaining what I needed so they brought it out for me to drink. The same happened when I had to pay. I got round the need to go into the restaurant that way and did not have to leave Honey in the car, so she got to sit in the sun with me. She also got the chance to get more and more used to being around people. This is what she needed, as where we lived there had not been that opportunity to mix the same way. Our hostess told me when I saw her when I got back that she, too, would be staying away that night and so I would be left alone with the workers who were building her extension. It was not something I wanted to hear, as I do have a fear of being attacked by men. I knew that this was an ideal opportunity to work with the fear, even though it was the last thing I expected. I knew in theory that I could lock the doors to the place we were staying in, but I could not lock the doors to the brain in the same way. There was nothing else I could do but deal with it. I did not want to finish the book. When you like a book that much it is hard to put down, and I wanted to leave some till morning. I could not escape that way. I had to go inward. And so I did. I struggled with the fear, telling myself that I was not being attacked at the moment and at my age they would surely not fancy me in that way at all. I kept repeating positive affirmations to get it out of the way and then went deeper and looked at what the attack was about. Because it has happened once it does not have to happen again, but it is still hard to get over. In 1996 I stayed with my friend Ann in Canada whom left me at her island home, while she went back to her other house in Vancouver, to deal with the same fear, but here all these years later it still could get hold of me, perhaps not as bad as it used to do but enough to make me feel uncomfortable in some circumstances. I finally got to sleep and woke to know that Howard was coming back that day and it was a lovely day. That night we had ordered a meal so we could celebrate his return and drink the champagne that had been left for us. I had asked for another meal to be made for my birthday. The hostess served us three courses and accompanying wine that worked really well with the meal. I enjoy being cooked for; it makes for a change and I enjoy checking out other people's ideas about food.

That morning Honey and I went to the nearest village again and this time did more exploring, wandering its back streets in the sunshine and again finding a new place to sit outside and have my treat of the day, a coffee. The coffee we had been drinking in Spain was excellent, so much better than the weak stuff we had at home. I suppose you do not realize it until you try something else, and it was clear that this was superior—I should say in most places. Later we went back to await Howard's call and he rang to say that he had been dropped off in the village we had been to earlier. It was great to go and pick him back up and take him to our temporary home among the grape fields. He had brought the mail that had been building up at his mother's and was pleased to be back in the warmth of Spain. We had a lovely evening chatting about our few days apart.

The next day was a Saturday and another lovely day. We went back to the village for a few things for the weekend and then went to a place called Santi Rubi. It was high in the mountains, and the information about it was correct,the views were fabulous and we could definitely see for miles. We left the car and in our happy state walked about admiring the place and the views. It was lovely in the sunshine, and we chatted and smiled and laughed, with Honey walking beside us. As we walked back to the car I noticed a little clump of valerian poking out from the bank. It grows well where we used to live, but I did not expect to see it here. That night we played a computer game and were amazed to have one of the objects to be valerian!

On Sunday we went out to lunch to a restaurant that had been recommended. We took a little while to find it, as the description of it was written backward. I went in to check and was told that it was full, but one of the waiters asked me when I wanted to eat and said that if we ate straight away we could have a table then. The food I chose was a bit rich, but it was a pleasant place and made a change to have lunch out.

It also gave us a feel of traditional Spanish life, as it catered mostly to the locals and was not set up like the tourist areas for the English. Later Honey got her usual lovely walk, and because it was so quiet we could let her off the lead so she could run through the grape fields. It is wonderful to see her run and enjoy the movement of her body. The trouble she has as of course we see it is she knows no real fears and is daft with people and cars and does not seem to take much notice of danger. She does not always do as she is told and come when we ask. She so loves life and people, but on that Sunday all went well and she could enjoy the freedom of that area. We were all very happy.

The next day was another day out. We only had two more days in Catalonia, so to make the best of it we set off for Montserrat. On the way I was stopped by a very friendly policeman who was doing a regular check on the traffic. I stopped the car and found my documents and supplied him with my passport. I did not get into any guilt trip with him, which was great, and all went well. As soon as he had seen my documents he stepped into the middle of the road and stopped all the traffic so I could get on my way and then gave me a friendly wave. Part of me wanted to ask him about the parking ticket and what I should do with it. But I refrained, knowing that I would sort it out somehow, some time.

We got to Montserrat without any hitch and found ourselves looking up at the amazing mountains. We stopped so Howard could take a photo of me clutching the dog, as his mother had seen one on the cover of the *Telegraph* magazine and thought it would make a good picture of me for her. We parked and I duly did my pose. A little way from us was a man with a very large camera who came over to ask us if we wanted to have a photo of all three of us with the impressive mountains as a backdrop. It turned out he was doing a BMW promotion and was a professional photographer. He was very kind and took some lovely photos of us. We thanked him and drove off to the tourist area of the mountains and again found ourselves in awe of the majesty of it all. Honey unfortunately had to stay in the car, but she had by then gotten used to her position in the back and did not complain too much. We went to check the place out and stare down the mountain into the valley below. Somebody felt so safe that they were walking on a wall as they chatted away to a friend. We both did not feel that action for us. We had felt exposed before, but here the roads were well maintained and a joy to drive. There was an interesting souvenir shop, so we went inside and visited the stalls all the way up to it. We bought cheese and honey and various other little treats to eat, and inside the shop I bought some fridge magnets to remind me of this very special day. On buying the magnets I realized that I had left one of my favorites back in Valencia when we were escaping the gas—obviously the priority was to get out and not worry too much about possessions. There was something about this place that had us chatting and smiling, and so we decided to stay for lunch there. I suppose the other thing about the day was that it was my last day at sixty-one, as the next day would be my birthday. I kept some of my food back for Honey so she also got a treat, and we walked back to the car. The journey down the mountain was again beautiful, but somehow we did not turn up where we thought we would. We kept getting lost and having to turn round trying to find the correct road. Over and over we kept missing the right road to turn in. We got into one town that was massive and could see no signs for our way home. At one point I stopped and asked a school patrolman. He pointed me in the right direction, and we eventually got onto the main highway through Spain. This was not what we hoped for, but we made the most of it. Yet we still went wrong and to our horror ended up in Barcelona Docks. There was one point in the whole procedure when Howard said the sun was setting over there and I knew I had to take control and use my intuition to get us home, so I headed west. Doing this I got onto the highway that took us back to the point where we had left it nearly ten days before and from there headed back to our latest home away from home. All this did not spoil our day, and when I got the photos on the laptop I was able to post them to various people so they could see where we had been. They all responded to the happiness on our faces, which was great to share.

My sixty-second birthday was on another lovely Spanish day. His mother had sent me a card via his trip to England, but because I was on the road I had little else to show that it was a special day. I did not mind, because the euphoria of the day before still hung on and we went out to the village for the last time. Sitting in the sun I rang my brother for a chat. He was complaining about the rain in England. It was good to hear him and know that I had not been totally forgotten. We went for our last walk with Honey and again enjoyed the area and the lovely views of the countryside around us. Our hostess who was cooking for me that evening presented a cake and some lovely rose cava so we could celebrate in style; all in all I felt very special. It was very kind of her, and then she presented the bill and told us that we needed to move the car early the next morning, as she had an excavator coming to dig up the yard. Consequently neither of us slept well as we were worried about sleeping in. It was as if all the timing was slightly skewed. Nothing of this bothered us too much, though, and we got the car repacked and I paid the bill by

Paypal. A couple of people had advised us that going through the Pyrenees at that time of year might be dangerous, but the road was clear of any snow and only the mountains held it high above us. Again the weather was glorious, and we were excited about our journey into France. We stopped for coffee on the way to the border and to give Honey yet another walk. We all now had to change languages and forget the Spanish we had learned. There were no border guards and no need for passports; just a smooth ride into another land. Our time in Spain was over, and a new adventure beckoned as we drove into France.

Chapter Four
FRANCE

Yes, the journey was over, or I should say through the Pyrenees was easy and it was lovely to see the mountains with snowy tips to them. There seemed little difference between Spain and France at that point, and why should it? It is only a boundary that divides them, and that is manmade and not anything else. We drove for a while before stopping for lunch. We were in high spirits at the ease of it all and finding a pleasant restaurant at the side of the road. We were the last to eat. They were about to close but said we could have the duck salad. So that is what we had, and it was very good too. It helped us feel a lot better about this leg of the journey, and we soon found ourselves approaching Narbonne. This time the hotel took dogs and we were able to walk her around the estate the hotel was built on so she got some exercise. The room was very good, and we were able to eat there and could relax and not have to hunt for somewhere to eat. I was able to get onto the Internet and ring up England so things that had been hanging about for a while could be sorted. I also got in touch with the woman who was going to give us the keys to the next property we were going to occupy, this time for two months, and arranged to meet her at lunchtime, as we were not sure how long it would take to get to the village where we were going to stay. The meal was good, and we had a bottle of wine to go with it. When we ate in a restaurant we had learned to put Honey back into the car so at least she was somewhere familiar rather than leave her in hotel bedroom that she has never seen before in her life. She travels very well and had spent an awful lot of time in the car over the last months, so it seemed the most sensible thing to do.

I did not sleep well, mainly because I think I was so excited at the prospect of being in France, but I had a good breakfast before hunting for the village. The road system again seemed to be relatively easy to follow, and we found ourselves getting there in good time. We found the house by going into the boulangerie in the village and asking for directions. The local bar was open, and we went in for a coffee. I was amazed that it was perfectly fine to take Honey in with us, as so many places in Spain had a sign outside to let us know that she was not welcome. The house was in the center of the village, tall and with a medieval courtyard yet full of modern gadgets we had to learn how to use. The woman who gave us the key was quick to leave as she had kids to pick up from school, so we made our own way around our own home. She added before she left that if we needed any help we only had to ring her and she would try to sort it. The kitchen was in the cellar, large but dark. It was very nice and so was the dining room next to it. You got out to the courtyard via there and up some steps, so it was actually at ground level. The sitting room and first double bedroom was on the first floor and above those two more double bedrooms, all with showers. The house had four toilets in all so no queuing there! We had to put the heat on in the sitting room and some of the bedrooms to warm the place up, as it had not been lived in for a while and was a little damp, especially because of its thick walls of ancient stone.

In the afternoon I took Honey on her first walk in the region. It was lovely to be still able to go walking without a coat in December. I had asked the woman who let us into the house and she had explained there were plenty of walks in the area. You just had to go a few minutes and you were in the countryside. She was right, and there we were walking down a lane in France admiring the banks and the grape fields at either side.

As much as I loved our new home I found that I still was not sleeping. I just could not get a full night's sleep. It went on for four nights until I got to the point where I really needed to go to one of the other beds we had to choose from and see if that helped. We had a lovely day in Pezenas finding the English bookshop and food from the market. Even in that state my intuition still worked and told me to go into a dress shop next door. There was the perfect jumper for me, and this is what Howard bought for my birthday. It was worth waiting for. It looked excellent with the clothes I had on, and you would think I had owned it forever. I was glad I had followed my instincts and made the purchase and was able to find the nearest town so easily. Life was looking up.

We had found out about the British bookshop by chance. I had noticed in the boulangerie a small magazine and took it home. It was free and was the Christmas edition. It was written in both English and French and told of a shop in our nearest town. We were very grateful for such a place; as nice as the house was there were no books or DVDs left there for us to use. This way we could at least have a book to read while we were there. I really enjoyed some of the books I had read while we were traveling about, especially the one in Catalonia. Here in the English bookshop I bought rather a splendidly written book about Cuba to take home. We also were able to buy Yorkshire tea there, something we needed, as we had run out of the tea we had brought with us. The tea we had bought in Europe had just been too weak for our taste.

Sleeping in the pretty front room was a problem for me. One of the windows had shutters, but the smaller window had no curtains at all. There was a curtain pole, so I hung a small curtain over it. But still the light from the street came through. I woke happy, but I just did not get enough sleep for my needs. We tried the back room with the mezzanine floor to see if that was any better. I slept okay, but this time Howard had the problem sleeping. I cooked a rabbit I had bought in the market with apple and rosemary, and it was delicious. It fed us for days. Each day I try a new mix of ingredients and then with the carcass made rabbit soup. Honey also enjoyed my culinary skills, so the rabbit did not go unappreciated.

We went again to Pezenas on Monday to find that most of the shops were shut. It was freezing cold to us now, not like the other day when we were able to go out in just a T-shirt. I pulled my coat around me and wished I had worn some warmer clothes. There was apparently snow in England, so we couldn't complain. My French was terrible; it seems the whole language part of my brain is mixed up. I had just been learning to talk in Spanish, and now I was in France and was talking in Spanish. I thought it was going to be easier, as I used to be at the top of the class at one time, but now my accent was so useless no one seemed to understand me at all. Of course all our books that we brought with us were for life in Spain. We had not bargained we would end up in France, so my French tapes and textbooks were in storage with all my furniture. We just have to muddle through and hope for the best. Luckily we are not deprived and got most things reasonably okay. I did find one perfumery open and bought some new skin cream, as my skin was looking a bit ropey with the little attention it had been getting lately. I had a very good deep cleanser and skin cream for the eyes and wondered if I could get something there. Luckily there was a special bargain price kit for the Christmas period sold as a gift set, so I bought that to try the stuff out. It seemed like a lot of money, but I did not really pay a lot for my upkeep so told myself I was worth it.

There is a problem with my PayPal account, and I was unable to pay the hostess from Catalonia. She started demanding even more money. I peered up at the screen and tried to resolve the problem. The Internet is marvelous when it works but like most things is infuriating when it does not and more and more patience is needed to sort it all out. We were also having problems learning to use the cooker and the induction hobs on top. I just did not seem to be able to get the hang of it, but we still managed as a couple to sort it out between us and get something cooked. I e-mailed the owner about how to use the cooker, as it did not work like the old electric cooker I got to know so well at the old house. Of course these are just teething problems, as they say, and would iron themselves out in due course.

The walks around the village were great for me and the dog; we loved them and wandered about happily each day. Howard came with us one day to look at the scary tree. All that was left of it was the trunk, and it has shaped itself into such a form that it looked like a man leering down at you as you walked along the lane. The first time we came across it, we were walking at dusk and were going to go further along the lane, but both the dog and I were struck by this curious tree and ventured no further that night. I took a camera to try to capture its evil stance over the lane. Howard saw at once what I meant, its gnarled trunk forming and bending to look down on us. This was our new home, and we loved it.

Other things were different here—the cuts of meat, for instance. I bought what seemed to be kidney, but what kidney I am not sure. It was only once I cooked it that I thought perhaps I should have done it another way. The dog got a very good dinner, and we ended up having cold chicken and salad. So much to learn, but never mind—we made the most of the experience, which is our way. I have also had to adapt to listening to the radio. I could not download TV programs, but I could still get radio and was able to listen to all of BBC radio instead. This I thoroughly enjoyed and listened to. I think I would probably have missed it if things were different. It is not that I particular liked watching TV. I had gotten out of that, as programs were so poor except for one or two things, and I didn't mind doing without. I am just happy I could listen to radio plays and music when the need took over. On came the headphones, and I traveled to another world.

The next day I got instructions on how to use the oven but was still having problems sorting the hob out. Even so I seemed to enjoy every day there, wandering the lanes with Honey and finding new routes to please us. The house was comfortable, and the courtyard was just lovely to sit in, as it seemed to be a sun trap. I had fixed a line across it so I could dry the clothes and gone out to buy pegs from the village shop. At first I had no idea how I was even going to get the clothes dry, but as usual I found a solution to my problem, and at night to finish off the drying process I put them on a heated towel rail and then the job was done. The washing machine had a marvelous fifteen-minute wash cycle, and as

I hate wasting energy and my things are never that dirty this seemed to solve the problem. I checked out my Louise Hay book for insomnia and recited the affirmation before I go to sleep. It seemed to work. It was a good affirmation and so would be doing some good along the way.

The next day we ventured out again. This time we went to the town known as Agde. It is the second oldest towns in France and is known for the material the cathedral is made of. It is near the sea, but we did not go as far as there. We found a car park at the edge of town and were the only ones using it. The walk in was lovely along the river and over the bridge. Blue skies and boats made the walk very attractive, and so out came the camera for me to record our journey. We found our way along the back streets; it certainly looked and felt old. Coming into a pretty square we were pleased to find a market going on with antiques or perhaps second-hand goods, as some might not be that old. There was some fascinating stuff there, and I ended up buying a very pretty glass vase to sit on the kitchen table. The kitchen needed flowers, and I was pleased with my purchase. There were lovely cafés to sit at and watch the market, so we had a coffee and later bought red candles for the candelabra, ready for Christmas. On the way back to the vehicle I saw some buildings painted onto a wall. They looked so real and were so attractive. They had done some things like that in Knaresborough but not on this scale, and so I took many photos. I was very impressed with the work; it was very clever. We walked back along the riverbank and found that our car was still alone in the park. In fact every time we went to Agde we were alone in this park. It was now our park, or so it seemed.

We usually spent one day exploring and one day at home doing the jobs needed and for me some writing. I found that the woman in Catalonia still had not gotten the money and so rang up PayPal and got the thing sorted out. Even when she got the money she wanted more. She wanted us to pay her costs. I didn't think so; it was not our place to do that. As much as we enjoyed our stay there it was very expensive for what it was, as all the attractions she offered were closed down for winter. We were getting the bare minimum facilities, and there was no heat for the first few days. Luckily we had come on our travels with three lovely blankets; would have been very cold without them. As much as it could be warm in the day the nights got quite cold, and these houses were set up for summer and not winter. It is a shame she was so greedy, as I would have been happy to advertise her place, but obviously her attitude needed some work. She was kind enough to bake a cake for my birthday, and I appreciated that, but she also charged us the earth for something that was not all that good a standard of accommodation. Of all the places we had stayed so far on this, our European tour, the first one was the best for comfort and things there to make life easy when you were staying in the house. It would win hands down in comparison with the others—what a shame the mountain road was so terrifying.

One of the other things to get used to were the hours shops were open. We went back into Pezenas for a bit more shopping and ended up popping to the pizza place when we got back to find that they had about finished serving. Certainly we could not sit there and have a meal, so we gave that idea up and in fact never went back. Neither of us was that keen on pizzas but thought about giving the local restaurant some money for food, as it is good to trade locally and keep small businesses going. It was warmer than our first visit to our local town, and it makes such a difference when you wander about not having to have scarves and hats and gloves in place. The village suited me, as I enjoyed wandering around the lanes and popping to the boulangerie for fresh bread and the caves for wine. I think the big blue skies helped too; no chance of SAD here. It was a full moon and an eclipse on Saturday, so I took another walk through the grape fields and watched the starlings perform their dance. A strange kind of peace took over as I took my place in the countryside. We had both started to sleep better too. Not that we really wanted to, but we tried separate bedrooms to see if that made a difference, as Howard preferred the front one and me the back. In the front the street light was just outside the bedroom window, and I found myself waking up thinking it was morning already. In the back I did not have that problem and just spread out in all the space I had to myself. When we all tried sleeping in that bedroom we found ourselves on the edge with bits of us touching the wood surround. That could be hard and off-putting, so this seemed the best solution, as we had three bedrooms to choose from. For me the third bedroom seemed smelly and damp and very poky too. That room had the best shower and was the one we ended up using, as the other showers were like being in a telephone box. Mind you it was strange that I chose the large room for me, but it was lovely opening the curtains each morning and watching the sun come up over the rooftops of the village. I could always read when I needed to and take up an early morning cup of tea and just sit up in bed and enjoy the thought of the approaching day. There was no CD player or TV in the house, but we were able to find other ways to enjoy ourselves. This place was also better for keeping in touch with friends back home, and that, too, made it a lot easier to be there.

One Sunday we visited Bessan. I thought it appropriate to do so, as it was my name in some ways. Bessan was on the way to Agde, so we had gone past it but had never ventured off the road to see what it was like. On first approach it did not seem such an attractive place, but we did see a market advertised and so left our car on the main street and walked to the center of the small town to the market. There were lots of lovely stores, and I ended up buying some lovely treats such as sun-dried tomatoes, dates and crystalized pears, and some lovely pink garlic and vegetables and lamb chops. When I went back to one stall to buy courgettes they were finishing off and packing up for the day so she would not sell me some, but a kind Moroccan man sold me some and added some celery too as a freebee. On returning home I managed to use the oven to cook a delicious lunch. It was more luck than anything else because even though they had sent us instructions for an oven it was not quite the same, so I just had to guess and hope for the best.

The next day would have been the birthday of our dear friend Graham if he had lived. We had bought a bottle of his favorite tipple to drink to his health, but somehow when the day came we just got on as usual and thought of him in our own special way. Howard had had another bad night's sleep, but I was full of energy and got up to do lots of little jobs, washing clothes and drying them in the sun in the courtyard, etc. We both agreed about how happy we were being in this place.

The next day we drove to Montpellier to check it out. It was not too far from where we were living and so did not take long to get to. At first we drove too far to nearly the other side before we found a place to stop. I asked a kind woman in a shop how to get to the old town, and she set me off back the way we came. Eventually I found it using my intuition, and we parked in an underground car park. The walk into the old town was just lovely, and I was struck by its beauty. I stopped for a salad, and we all sat outside to watch and check out the lovely architecture around us. The shops were beautiful, and as we got further into the center we were struck by all the lovely Christmas decorations everywhere. I was in my element in this beauty and took loads of photos but somehow just did not capture it on camera. There were loads of stalls full of people everywhere and so much to see. We wandered down side streets exploring and taking in the elegance and beauty and having various cups of coffee. I ventured into one small shop and bought myself some lovely white Christmas decorations. They were so very pretty I could have bought loads but stopped myself and just bought about four. We went home via the country route, not using the main motorway. The problem was that with all the energy I used on Monday and the journey around Montpellier I was exhausted when we got home and so ended up being ill the next day and stayed in bed trying to get over it all. It was a big reminder that I needed to keep the stress down and look after myself well. We had lots of time to explore, and I didn't need to do everything all in one day. But the trip had been worth it, as I will always remember the amazing architecture and the beauty and joy of our day out.

One of the great points about not having what you need in one way was to find something else to amuse yourself. There was no DVD player or DVDs, just some contraption for seeing films with no instructions. My main source of entertainment became the BBC radio downloads. My fascination with the human psyche had me listening to a wonderful French woman's story, a woman who drove a Bugatti. Her story was really interesting, and like a lot of women I admire she was before her time and broke the rules. There were also lots of good plays to listen to, and rather than see the characters as someone else portrayed them I was able to make them up in my own mind. We also found YouTube to be a great help, and one evening we both watched a story on Byron in several parts that someone had kindly put on from the BBC. All this helped no end, and I was able to travel again to the nearest town to check out the various shops there for food and other provisions. Both of us love reading and were able to enjoy this with help from the English shop in Pezenas, which had second-hand English books for sale and strong tea. The woman who ran the shop was very pleasant, and it was a good experience to visit her. I bought a tiny Christmas tree from her, too, which will come in handy year after year. It was very sweet. When one of us went into a shop the other would hang outside with Honey, as she enjoyed the smells and watching people go by. This Saturday was particularly cold, and so lots of clothes were needed for getting around; yet we managed. The weather seemed to have one day cold and two days warm. The cold pierced you after having the warmth because we had gotten out of the habit of thinking cold in some ways. One day I had bought veal for Sunday lunch and made a breadcrumb and herb surround for it, as there was little fat and I felt it needed something to keep the flavor in. I had bought it from a butcher and so had to make up the recipe, as I could not find one suitable on the Internet. Most recipes were for thin strips of veal rather than the chunk I had bought. It was another cold miserable day, but I did get it cooked. I was disappointed in the flavor, wishing I had not left my French cookbooks in storage. I am not sure how I feel about veal cooking, as apparently it has got better for the male cows they destroy for this type of meat. The whole question of eating meat is up for debate with some people being strongly against eating flesh, prefering a vegetarian diet while others believing we are all equal. The fact that plants feel, too, makes me wonder what really we should be doing for the best.

And then there is the question about the dog—what should she eat? Is she doing wrong by eating flesh too? Honey would answer that question with a resounding "No." Unfortunately, as the veal joint was rather small, there was not a lot left for her to try out.

Christmas was nearly on us, so I went on the Internet and sorted out some Christmas greeting cards via Jacquie Lawson and sent them all around the world. It is well worth the money and saved quite a few trees I am sure.

The next day we attempted yet another trip out, this time went to Beziers. I had not slept well again, but we got there and back in one piece even with a mistake at a junction where Howard thought the red light was for another lot of traffic and not us. We got through unscathed and left the car at the side of the road and walked into the center. It was another miserable day, and the whole town seemed unaware that it was Christmas at the weekend. If we had been in England the place would have been swarming with people shopping, but here there were few shops open and very few people about either. In some ways I prefer this to the overcommercialization of Christmas that we have in England. It somehow now blunts the original ideas for festivals at this time of year and we end up looking at competition and how many presents you get. It is a very stressful time of year rather than a time for slowing down and enjoying the dark nights and short days and letting things go for a while.

We came home for lunch, and in the afternoon I listened to a talk on vulnerability. The speaker had come to the same conclusion as me—that it was important to notice one's feelings and not run away from them. If you did the latter you missed both the good and the bad. I try to do this and stay with those scary feelings and then give myself time to see what is behind them. I, of course, don't always succeed, but it is good that there are more people looking at life like this and enabling us to move to love from fear.

I tried to rest as much as possible to get over the pains and tiredness I had been feeling, wandering about with the dog in the afternoon and exploring the area but generally not pushing myself too much. There were two public gardens in the small village, so the dog and I explored them. They were not particularly inspiring but made a nice afternoon wander. I found it hard to get over the clear blue skies and the peace of the area after the bustle of England and its numerous people. The locals usually called "bonjour" as I wandered by, but this afternoon I hardly saw a soul as I walked among the modern houses; perhaps their owners were out at work.

On Wednesday we went back to Agde to the outdoor second-hand market to buy our Christmas presents. We bought little presents to remember the day by. I ended up with a handbag in red and blue that I chose, as Howard saw nothing that he thought was appropriate. I bought him an interesting pot and a little watercolor painting that seems just right as a present from France. He had pointed out the pot to me on the way round, so I knew he liked it. I think he was going to buy it for me, but really the bag was something I could use all the time. I had two good bags—well, three—but I couldn't resist the shape of this one and it was Parisian, so that made me feel good about the design. I wouldn't have it to unwrap, but his mother had sent me something that I would keep till the holiday. We walked back to the car and sat on the seat overlooking the river and took in the beauty. There was a lovely peace about it all.

It was solstice, and I sent messages to friends to enjoy this time. Of course we probably should have built a big fire and danced around it and had a drink to the season, but here in this house where everything was electric and far away from the land in some ways it was inappropriate. I just acknowledged it and hoped for a time when it was okay to do so. My friend Janet had the space for a bonfire and so would be making the most of it. Howard was now the one suffering from feeling rubbish, so I went out to do the shopping. My confidence in driving in France had gone a bit with him sitting beside me, so it was good that I was going on my own. I managed perfectly well and parked in a new area, which enabled me less hassle than before. It was a lovely day for taking photos. With all the pretty Christmas decorations I hoped for some good pictures. Unfortunately the memory stick was still in the laptop, so that was a total flop. I decided that I would just have to try again another day.

Christmas drew nearer, and somehow I look at Facebook and found lots of messages for my birthday. It kept changing things round, so I never saw them on the day. It was good to hear from people around the world and know we can be close that way even if it is via the Internet. At last we both felt a lot better and celebrated the shortest day and looked forward to the celebration in front of us.

I suppose it is a frame of mind, what were we celebrating. The old ideas are never mentioned, and the birth of Christ hardly gets a mention either, but I cooked what turned out to be a guinea fowl stuffed with mushrooms and flavored with brandy plus all the other accompaniments associated with this time of year. We had opened our presents earlier and rang Betty to thank her. She had bought me a cashmere scarf and a centerpiece for our Christmas table along with serviettes to match. It looked just right with all the other things I had decorated the table with and so was a good addition to the many bits and pieces I now had. I especially loved the white decorations that hung in the sitting room making it so pretty. Later in the day I walked the dog around the grape fields and noticed again how at peace I was in this area. As we did not have a television there was no sitting around a roaring fire stuffed to the gills and watching it in a trance. We made the most of the circumstances and entertained ourselves.

There were some lovely walks around the area. One day I found myself at an electricity substation but could not go any further and had to turn back. But there were lovely views of the surrounding area. The village policeman drove by and waved as we walked back home, and partridges flew over my head. I also had to learn to make new things to eat and experiment with my own recipes, as I could not find anything on the Internet that would work with my own ingredients. I realized that I had bought quail and stuffed them with a mixture of shallots and crystalized pear and clementine, etc. It seemed to work, but I was not sure about eating quail and probably won't try it again. Howard ate up yesterday's guinea fowl while Honey got to eat a little bit of everything! As I said before we had not reckoned on France and there was no dictionary at hand, so shopping sometimes ended up being a case of luck. If I did not recognize the food I was buying I might just end up with anything. I do not know what I was thinking when I bought the quail, and with an oven that did not make sense. The fact that we got to eat was a gift in a way, because I could have easily burned everything to a crisp. Hearing from friends also made this time of year special, bringing us closer together with all the memories.

Even though I loved France and had decided I wanted to live there I found myself not feeling too good in the house, and the lack of sleep kept coming up. One day I didn't seem to be able to feel warm and so took it very gently again. I wanted to go down to the sea, but my health stopped that so we put it off for another day. When we did go I was glad we had waited. We got to Se^te for the first time and found a parking spot and then walked to the center of the town. It was a beautiful day with a lovely blue sky, and we wandered along staring at the sea and the sky and the mosaic that has been placed along the walk to make it even more attractive. I loved looking at the harbor and the boats and found a place for a coffee that was just right. Honey sat but got fussed over by the restaurant staff. She took it all in her stride. We people-watched together before exploring further and came across a big outdoor market along with an indoor market where I bought some ham. There was so much to look at again, and I took photos of the pretty bandstand covered with decorations. Honey did not even notice a dog eating a huge bone, as there are so many amazing smells for her to check out.

I felt that it was time to stop for a bite to eat. Some people passed us as we sat in the café. Their clothes stood out, as they wore rather smart outfits complete with matching hats. I noticed that they were eating two restaurants away and were still there when we had explored the market and shops. We chose that café to eat at, and I had a salad and a kir for a change, Howard had some wine while Honey looked on.

We all came back highly satisfied with our day out.

The next few days were quiet, and we do not go far from our base. I did not sleep well again and dreamt a lot when I did sleep. I took Honey on her usual walks and noted the synchronicity in my life. One of the most interesting examples I noted was writing on page 11:11 about noting the time of 11.11 on the 11th day of the 11th month of 2011. It was something I never seem to get over when I notice the wonder of it all. I had one last night that was interesting: a friend mentioned the French Resistance, and then listening to a radio program they mentioned it as well. It was just like when I dreamed of a friend and another radio play mentioned where she lived. It was not an ordinary place at all, but there it was in December just like it happened yesterday. And so the year ends with our enjoyment of France and each other and having such lovely times. I did not make any New Year's promises to myself. For some reason there was not anything that I felt I needed to do better, not that I am perfect but just happy with how things are.

On New Year's Day the sun shone and it was so warm that we were able to sit outside and have lunch in the courtyard at the back of the house. It seemed a perfect start to a new year, and again later in the day I wandered through the fields with the dog, the blue sky being a perfect backdrop to our walk. That evening an e-mail came from Hawaii from my friend Ann and her husband Paul stating that they were our Canadian family. I feel so loved now; what more is there?

Chapter Five

FRANCE IN JANUARY

S leep was still a problem even one month later. If it was not one of us it was the other. We still tried to explore and make the most of our stay. On Wednesday we went back into Se^te and went around the market again. The weather was breezy when we set off, yet when we got there it was calm and beautiful. This time we parked closer to the edge of the town so we did not have so far to walk with our purchases. Today I made a change to my makeup, I realized that it was time to soften the look with brown mascara instead of black and a sage green shadow to go better with my eyes. I don't want that look of desperation that takes over when you get to a certain age and feel you need to try to look younger. People seem to get stuck in a certain look that worked at one time but as you age it really does not have the same effect and looks tired and aged. For me it was an experiment to see how it felt to be a certain way. Who am I in all this?

I still did not think things had cleared from the fumes in November and decided that I would need a checkup when we got back to England. It could be psychosomatic. It was the car that reminded me when I saw a strange light coming on and wondered what that was about at the same time seeing two cars giving off a lot of fumes. I checked to see if there was a message there and made the decision to look after myself better. Could our strange sleep patterns be connected with the building or with what had happened? Howard was down and tired and did not want to go anywhere, so I ended up doing all the shopping and taking the dog for a while. I loved the walks but couldn't help worrying about Howard. The positive side of all this was that I started to get my confidence back for driving in France. It was eroded a bit with not doing much driving on my own, I suppose. Of course I was used to doing that in the past, but as a family it takes on a whole new shape.

Luckily, by Saturday Howard started to feel a lot better and we went to Vias to the beach. We were alone even though it was supposed to be one of the best beaches in the south of France. On the way all the shops that would have been very active in the summer season were closed and barred. It was odd to see them like that, but it meant that we can let Honey off the lead on the beach and let her run. She had a ball of a time, and so did I. Both of us like to run, and with all that freedom we both went for it. I couldn't believe the luck we had to have all this space to ourselves, but we did and we all made the most of it. Howard played with Honey and tossed her things to run after. She loved the game and tried to get an old buoy from the sea. I gathered shells and just enjoyed being in the lovely environment. It did us good, and we ended up having a lovely weekend with lots of pleasant food. I enjoy the creativity of cooking as well as everything else, and the others made the most of my skill. The year was starting well, and with the Internet I was able to listen to various predictions for our future. Some felt right, but others did not jell at all. I was learning how far I had moved internally and had grown and healed.

On Monday I went to Carsaconne on my own, because Howard was not up to going all that way. I was in need of exploring and took the road to Pezenas and followed the signs to Narbonne. Some of the road I had been on before, but after Narbonne it was totally new territory. It seemed perfectly straightforward, so I was not worrying. I felt sad that Howard was not able to accompany me, but I knew I needed to do this for myself and look at more of the country while I was here. As I turned north after Narbonne the world got greener and I had large plains on either side of me. It was lovely to drive through the French countryside, and there were again blue skies. I found the town quite easily and drove into the center and parked. It was as pleasant as I expected. I had not gotten into the old town but more into new part where the shops were. The really old part I found on the way out. I walked to the center and looked at the shops and then found a place for a hot chocolate. It was not all that warm, but the café was friendly and I was able to sit back and watch the other patrons. I did not stay long, as I did not need to. I had gotten there and explored enough, and I felt better for making the effort. I was so full of energy when I got back that I took Honey a long walk, so we both got a lot out of the day.

The weather was very changeable. The next day was so warm that I felt the sun burning my body and was able to open all the shutters and windows so the sun would come in. The next day it was cold, so I needed a large jumper, coat, scarf, and gloves to keep me warm. I went to the market in Agde. With the freezing air around us there was no stopping for coffee, but I was able to buy some pretty ribbon for a friend's birthday. What a contrast. That day I started to organize our journey back to England and book hotels so Honey could stay with us. The first place we booked was Limoges. I thought it would be useful to be in that area because we had seen some lovely places to buy there and the house we hoped to rent for the spring was not far away. They would take the dog, and I had parking, too, which would stop me from worrying about all our possessions left in the car. First of all I thought we should go toward Paris, but then I realized that we could stay in Chartres, which would give me a chance to look at the cathedral that is so famous for its rose windows and labyrinth, etc. There was a hotel close by that took dogs. I found it interesting that in France it was much easier to find hotels for Honey than in Spain. We do not really like leaving her in the car all night. I just hoped the journey there would go well and we wouldn't lose our booking as we did before when we got lost in Spain.

Another day when we visited Narbonne I wasn't feeling great again, but I liked looking at the center with its canal and old market building. Again there seemed a need to make the place look attractive and inviting. It was cold again, so we didn't stay long. The internet said Narbonne was interesting , but maybe we had gone to the wrong area, because I could not see myself going back again. I am glad I went, though, and so don't feel I missed anything. On the way home I took a wrong turn. Well, what I mean is I did not get off the main road when I should have and there was not a place to get off for miles. We ended up driving far too long and I got tired and irritated by my mistake. I am hard on myself and realize that I should not be so mean and cranky at mistakes. The trouble is if I think about the map I feel I should have known better, but perhaps we all feel that now and again.

America was trying to come up with a reason for bombing Iran again. How can we expect wars not to happen when we attack ourselves so badly? I must be kinder to myself. I repeat it: *I must be kinder to myself.*

It was announced at the weekend that it was my famous distant relative's seventieth birthday on Sunday. It is amazing how he does it; according to doctors he should have been dead in his twenties. I did not suppose I would ever meet him now, but when I went walking with the dog I saw hawks in the distance. It seemed appropriate with our family name like that of a hawk and my immediate family's love of raptors.

The weather changed again, and it was now warm enough to eat out again. The day before we had explored the antique shops of Pezenas. We enjoyed it, but we were not sure about Honey. I wanted a big house to decorate with some of the lovely and strange things they had for sale. The town was known for its antique shops, and there were certainly lots of them. I fell in love with an ornate bird cage but reminded myself that we had to go back to England soon and space was the premium.

I felt better now that I had found us a place for March through to May. The thought of leaving France for good was too much, and we decided that we needed to return in an attempt to find our perfect home. We decided that we might as well make a base here and look around rather than trying to do that from England. There was one place in Brittany that I was not sure about, but the other place had an acre of orchard and sounded so much better. We decided to go for it. I needed now to send yet another down payment to secure it. This was another lesson in trust and faith. Oh dear, as I go for it yet again. Luckily this time the woman was easy to speak to and came from not far from us in North Yorkshire while the man I spoke to sounded distant and not that interested. I went with the woman.

Mid-week we visited Clermont; it was not far away, and we wanted to see a more inland town. There was a lake close by, but we chose to go there another day. I wanted to see the French countryside before we left, but that day we just wandered around the little town admiring the architecture and had lunch outside again. I was too excited to sleep much the night before at thoughts of our new home in the spring. The people had the same names as a couple I used to know; the woman had an affair with my ex. We realized that it could not be the same people and laughed at the idea. I checked my feelings and realized that I had no anger or resentment toward her and was grateful for that. That was then and now is now, and my life was so much better with my husband than with the ex. The orchard of our new property excited me, and all that space. We were enjoying the south of France, but space was tight and we loved the land, so it suited us so much better than where we were. I couldn't help panicking—well, just a little—that the whole thing might fall apart and leave us without anywhere to live, but I reassured myself that it will be all right and got my faith back in this whole adventure.

The next time we were in Pezenas I made the most of the January sales and went in a lingerie shop to inquire about getting a new bra. It was not something I had done for a while, and I decided that it was time I spent more money on my appearance. It must have been something in the air, or perhaps just being in France gets you to do that, as they are known for their lingerie and taking time over their looks. I thought I had lost weight since Spain and was pleased to be told I was down one dress size and now needed a smaller bra. The bra and knickers sets were so beautiful I couldn't help feeling beautiful too. I ended up buying one set but coveted another set and after a lot of thought decided to go back for the other one another day. Two at once seemed just so extravagant, but then I reminded myself that I am worth it. I took the first set home and wore it feeling wonderful and glad to know I had lost weight without much effort. It must have been the dog walking, but could it have been something else? I tried not to worry.

Again we took Honey to the beach and had a run, and this time she knocked me down onto the sand. She ran so close that sometimes she would take me with her. This was the second time I landed on my backside, and luckily I did not get hurt in the falling. I found myself laughing at my situation, sitting on the damp sand. It was a lovely day, and I was so lucky to be able to run and enjoy myself that way. I gave thanks for this gift. Honey did not want to stop; she loved it there running and playing on the beach beside the Mediterranean. She ran into the sea after a stone and got out of her depth and swam for the first time. It was a wonderful moment for us all, but I feared that when Honey got overexcited it was hard to stop her and she could get into trouble. It took a lot of coaxing back onto the lead when it was time to go home. I made a decision: if the white embroidered bra was still there when I went back to the shop in a few days' time I would buy it. Why not? It did fit perfectly and look and feel so good when I tried it out in the shop.

The next few days went along in a happy contented way with us just enjoying ourselves in France and being part of our own little family. The weather changed from day to day; one day the sun came out and the clothes came off and the next day we found ourselves putting them all on again. I found myself enjoying the radio again and the connections I found on the Internet, so even though we were away from each other we could share our experiences.

Later on in the week we went to the countryside and to the lake, the one near Clermont we did not visit the other day. It was a lovely day with gorgeous blue skies but was still cold. There were not many people about because it was so early in the year and before any type of holidaying takes place. I took photos of the lovely place we were experiencing. Honey was a big part of our walk and found the water fascinating again, but this time we kept her on the lead. I was glad we had made the effort to look at this place and take time in nature again. At night we found out more about our new home in France and got excited by the photos that had been sent to us. It all looked so lovely; it was hard not to want to be there right then.

The next day I found a dead scorpion in the sink. I believed it to be a sign and soon got an e-mail from a friend who is a Scorpio. Then in the evening after hearing a donkey in the village I saw that *Travels with a Donkey* by Robert Louis Stephenson was on the radio. In listening to it I realized that it was not unlike the book I was attempting to write. I felt that was a very good motivator and was pleased to have taken time to listen to it. I saw my *Travels with Honey* as a modern-day version.

Another day we decided to go to Marseillan and check the place out. I fell in love with the little town. The sky was a wonderful blue, and everything looked lovely. It seemed absolutely perfect. I was so happy there, and enchanted. We decided to come back for our Sunday lunch and take in this place again. We wandered around and took in the sea and the pretty little town, so much fun. There was a beautiful boat in the harbor, and I took a photo. The colors were magnificent against the sky. That Sunday it was a lot colder but I still enjoyed being there. Although we had a lovely Sunday lunch the restaurant was not heated so it spoiled our day out. I just did not have enough clothes on, and the café was not very warm. I realized how much I liked being warm. Did I notice the cold because I was older? Or was I so used to being warm that I only noticed the cold days?

Suddenly it was time to leave this house in France, bags to be packed and the whole house cleaned. I did it bit by bit so I was not put off by it all. I dusted and washed the floors and tidied up. There were some things we had hardly used in this all electric world, like the microwave—we tend to keep it simple. The agent was coming the next day in the morning to pick up the key. She was not at all interested in us in the beginning, but now it seemed she was friendlier. I can't help wondering if it was because we wanted to buy a house and she might make a sale. When she did get to the house she said she won't bother to look around. She said she was "sure it will be all right." In hindsight we wish we had made her look round, as the owners came up with a list of things we could not argue about. That was if we wanted to get some of the deposit back at all. But that day we did not know any of that and took her word and drove off into the north with all of our things back in the car. It was cold again, but we were happy and making our way to Limoges. I did not realize how far it was and how long it would take, but Honey got a walk before we set off and each time we stopped. The roads were excellent, so we used the toll roads and stopped for food and drink and diesel now and again. It was quite exciting to be on the road again, but I could not help wondering if it was going to snow. It felt so much like it, and as we got further north there were traces of it at either side of the road. We were lucky it did not come down while we were driving. The places we stopped for drinks and snacks were very smart, and most had water connected to them. One had a moat-like structure around and was attractive. There were easy places to walk Honey. I loved looking at the countryside and the woods that accompanied us as we drove north. I was happy with it all.

We did not get to Limoges until about five at night, just when it started to get busy, but found the center and eventually a person to point us in the right direction for the hotel. I went in to check where we could put the car and was given a card for the garage, as it was under the hotel or through it. We were so glad we booked the parking, as it means all our things were safe within the hotel grounds. I asked the receptionist to book us more parking in Chartres. I did not want to worry about all our possessions that were heaped up in the back of the car. It were very cold and there was no restaurant, but they did room service and so we went for that. The thing with room service was that we did not have to go out and leave Honey anywhere. It was far too cold to leave her in the car, and we were all snug in the hotel bedroom. It was a great big hit, and we enjoyed ourselves having this luxury with a bottle of wine. We were safe and could sleep not worrying about anything. Breakfast, too, was good. We took turns over breakfast so we do not have to leave Honey alone in the room. She had not ever been left alone in a strange place, and we were not going to start then.

I do not know what I expected of Limoges, but my thoughts about exploring were overtaken by the extreme cold. We were all so cold it was nearly hard to think. I asked how to get to the center of the town, and we easily found our way from the instructions. It looked rather interesting, but it was hard to stand still and stare, as the cold was getting to us. I rushed into a shoe shop with a sale on for some warm boots and later bought a hat for the same reason. Howard, I realized, was getting sick from the cold, so I ran like a mad woman into another store to buy him a warm scarf and another for gloves. I felt like I was being possessed, as I was acting out of character in an endeavor to get warm. We soon gave up the sightseeing after buying a present for his mum, which is what we had hoped for in the first place, and walked back to the hotel. They had not finished doing our room, so they gave us free coffees in the lounge while we waited. We bought brandies to go with them just to help us feel better again. It had been a shocking experience, so we ended up not leaving the hotel room for the rest of the day. Room service came into play again. We tried a variety of things from the menu, and the car stayed safely in the parking place close by.

The next day we headed out again and further north to Chartres. The drive was not so bad, and we got there in good time to explore the town. The parking place was not as good as it was a little way from the hotel but was locked at night with a big gate. It was nearly full when we got there, but we were able to get in and leave our keys again with the receptionist. He was very helpful, and we had another nice room. There was a pool and spa at this hotel, but first we went looking around the center and then to the cathedral. I had wanted to see the labyrinth, but that area was being done up so I missed it; perhaps I would see it at a later date. I took photos of the area, and we noticed that Honey was being aggressive to other dogs. Her usual pleasant nature was really lost for a time, and she even started barking and being nasty to a huge Irish wolfhound. Nothing seemed to faze her at all; she is quite an amazing dog. Again because the car park was away from the hotel and it was still too cold to leave her in the car and we did not want to leave her alone in the hotel bedroom, my little black dress stayed in the bag and we had room service again. It is not quite the same as having a romantic meal in a restaurant, but there was nothing we could do about it given the circumstances and the weather, so we ate in the room again. It was an excellent meal, and we all did well—especially Honey, who had some rather nice steak, leftovers of course.

The weather got worse the next day as we made our way to Calais, but luckily now we did not have far to go. Howard got in a total muddle about directions, but the hotel receptionist helped by giving us the best way to go from Chartres. We had to go via Rouen, a place I had been to fifteen years before. I am sure I would never have guessed all those years ago that I would be driving around the city with my husband and dog in tow. We found the port quite easily, but getting a ferry was not going to work out as I had envisaged it. One look at Honey's passport and we were told we had to get her injected and then wait twenty-four hours before she could go back to England. We now had to drive round the town and hunt for the vet. Howard seemed lost again, and I felt stressed at my plans going awry. I was worrying that if we did not get to the vet in time we would be stuck in Calais for a lot longer. It was Saturday afternoon and they probably would not work Sundays, so we could be here ages if we did not get her seen shortly. We eventually found it and got the jab, so now we had to find a hotel for the night. The first one was not okay at all, so I drove around till I found one on the edge of town, again paying a little more so at least our possessions would be safe and of course one that took dogs. The roads were slippery with ice, but we got there and waited for the next day.

The room was cold but heated up a little. I had a bath because I was feeling the stress of it all, and with one look at the bed we realized that Honey was now in heat. Had the strain been too much for her as well? A little more patience was needed.

The next morning I found myself driving on snow and making my way back to the port and to the ferry. The hotel had provided a very miserable breakfast on such a cold day. I had expected a lot better, as at another hotel in the same chain we had an excellent assortment of food to choose from. This was awful in comparison. I was very grateful to have the four-by-four to drive to the port, as it was icy and not an easy drive. None of the snow had been cleared, so we were sliding about trying to park; well, not us, but most of the other cars that came to get the ferry. I went in to get the tickets and hand over the documents from the vet. All was well and we were finally able to get on the ferry and go back to England. A kind man on the ferry gave us a special place to park, as it would be freezing cold on the ferry for Honey. Luckily it was a very short journey across the channel so it was not too bad for her, and before long we were at Dover and it was my turn in the passenger seat.

Howard took over the driving, and I now became the navigator. This was a totally different experience for me, as I had been the one driving us around Europe for over four months.England is different from the rest of Europe and people drive on the left hand side of the road, he was used to driving on the left whereas I had got used to driving on the right in that time. Now I had to let go and let someone else take over the driving and the act of us getting us home safely. I was determined not to be a back-seat driver. It is something I dislike in others, so I was hoping I would not be one either. I managed fine even though I noticed that I was leaning to the right all the time. I had to keep pulling myself up and adjust my seat. It was a weird sensation, although I was very grateful not to be driving, as the weather was atrocious, with freezing fog and every other condition you could think of. Howard is a marvelous driver and did amazingly considering he had not driven for over seven years due to illness and lack of confidence. We stopped once for a meal, as it was going to be too late to start eating when we got home and let Betty know our whereabouts and to not worry about providing anything for the weary travelers. We got there late on Sunday night, traveling all the way from Dover. In a way it was good to be back, and Betty made us feel very welcome. It had been a long, tiring journey, and we had covered a lot of ground. We went to bed relieved that we were safe and sound and slept well in the little bedroom with Honey. We were all together, and it was great.

Chapter Six
MAYBE

The time back in England went very fast. The first few days were spent just taking in everything that had happened over the last few months and getting over the long journey home. For me everything now was different, with my meals being cooked for me and not having to do anything in the house but meet friends and have lunches out with them or tea and cake, whatever the case may be. Howard went to see his consultant, and that went well. Betty had her eye operation, and she was fine too. It was good that we were in the house for her, as it was quite a frightening prospect to have an operation on your eyes even though everybody said it was quite straightforward and easy. Of course all operations can go wrong, so it is not that reliable to believe that you are going to go though it without any issues. I was out most days doing something and organizing what needed to be arranged so we could go back to France at the end of February. I also had a check-up to see if the gas had effected me, had my teeth cleaned and my eyes checked. All were fine so I felt very lucky that there had not been too much damage done on the way. There was also Honey to walk and get her out without male dogs taking advantage of her state. Somehow we managed it all without too much hassle, and before long we were back on the road to France. Honey is such a good little dog and takes so much in her stride, including not having the freedom of the backyard. She seemed to bleed for an awfully long time this time, so we covered all the settees, floors, and beds so she did not stain anything. It took me back to my own moontimes all those years ago and the strangeness of it all when blood seemed to appear from nowhere and leave you with awful pains and discomfort. Not the best of times for a woman, and I am not sure all that great for a dog/bitch. I left England feeling very loved and cared for and glad that I had been able to see so many friends and enjoy their company.

We spent the last night in England in Ramsgate with a hotel overlooking the harbor. It was very nice, and we were able to enjoy a delightful evening there with a bottle of wine outside and fish and chips, watching the inhabitants wander to and fro. This meant the next morning after an excellent breakfast we were able to go to the ferry relatively easily and get one straight away before we took on the journey to our new home. The price of the ferry crossing was a lot dearer than the time before, but that was probably because we were going early in the morning and not on a Sunday. This time it was less taxing for Honey, and we were now on yet another adventure on a journey we both could share. When I got tired Howard drove, and vice versa.

We kept telling our hosts the time of arrival, as they were cooking us a meal, and slowly, our so it seemed, we edged nearer to our destination. We finally arrived and were greeted warmly by them. It was dark by then, so we only saw the inside of our new home. It was really lovely and welcoming, with a huge wood-burning stove in the old kitchen. It was a real farmhouse kitchen and a pleasant place to be. We were given wine and a lovely coq-au-vin to eat and a lovely big bed to sleep in. The hosts retreated to the other end of the house and left us there to sleep soundly after our long day traveling. It was the next day that held us in awe as we opened the curtains and looked at the orchard behind the house. It was magnificent and even more so, as the woodland at the other side of the wall belonged to the house. I was in love; in fact we both were. We had found our home at long last, and by the end of the day we had decided we would be here for a year at least.

It is a place where we could really relax and give Honey loads of space for running and enjoying lots of new smells. It gave us all what we need.

The question is how did we get here? Was it purely following my intuition? I do not have the answers, but taking the trail I did and the experiences in Spain had been a pilgrimage of sorts, a modern-day pilgrimage.

To quote Satish Kumar: "We can relate to our planet Earth in two ways. Either we can act as tourists and look at the Earth as a source of goods and services for our use, pleasure and enjoyment, or we can act as Earth Pilgrims and treat the planet with reverence and gratitude. Tourists value the earth and all her natural riches only in terms of their usefulness to themselves. Pilgrims perceive the planet as sacred, and recognize the intrinsic value of all life.

"To be a pilgrim is to be on a path of adventure, to move out of our comfort zones, to let go of our prejudices and preconditioning, to make strides towards the unknown. If we want to tread the pilgrim's path, we need to go beyond ideas of good and evil, and to be dedicated to our quest—to our natural calling. We need to shed not just our unnecessary material possessions but also our burdens of fear, anxiety, doubt and worry; in this way we can find spiritual renewal and enter on the great adventure of the unknown. Paradoxically, being on a pilgrimage doesn't necessarily mean traveling from one place to another—it means a state of mind, a state of consciousness, a state of fearlessness.

"At this critical stage of human history we need a new kind of pilgrim, unattached to any form of dogma—'Earth Pilgrims' who are concerned with this world, not the next, and who are seeking a deep commitment to life in the here and now, upon this earth, and in this world. We need to realize we are all connected, and through that connectivity we become pilgrims.

"As pilgrims we learn to celebrate the beauty and the bounty of the earth and develop a sense of gratitude for all the gifts of life and that we receive. The Sacred Earth is a gracious host to all pilgrims. If we live a simple and elegant life there will be enough in the world for everybody's need, as there can never be enough for everybody's greed."

In reality I had become a pilgrim in 1998 when I said to myself that I would try things out in a different way and follow my heart instead of my head. It had led me on many adventures in the States and all over the planet, but I did not know really what I was doing at the time. When I sold my house at the age of fifty and ended up in Arcosanti for a while I found an article there about Satish Kumar. I did not know I would meet him many years later and ask him if I was a pilgrim. He answered "yes" to that question. In his talk about life he mentioned going on pilgrimages at age fifty, which is what I had done, but again I had not known the real reason at all. I was very lucky to have been able to do such a thing, but it took me to many places in my head that needed changing so I could find myself again. I wonder sometimes whether if I knew at the beginning what I would encounter I would have set out on such a journey that seemed to take such a long time. There I was wandering about hunting for a home and an answer to my many questions that made sense. I found lots of resentment and arrogance mixed up with a certain pride and vanity. These were not easy things to look at. Anger came up very early, even before the start, so maybe it was lurking about for ages waiting to show itself to me. It can be so frightening to notice. As a child and then as a grown-up I was terrified of making others angry and so become a "yes" person. That, too, is equally awful when you think of all the fear behind it and the inability to show your true feelings and say "NO." This took a long time to deal with, as it was so hard for me to change, but when I got ME, also known as chronic fatigue syndrome, that helped a lot and helped me to start to heal that part of me.

Perhaps it would have been a shorter journey if I had had a particular master or guru to help me though, but that wasn't my path. I looked for gurus all the time originally, but listening to my heart it would take me to them and then take me away before I got too attached. Somehow I had to find it myself. Hence I have no real dogma and enjoy looking at all sorts of ideas to find the kindest way forward. I can thank Tom Brown Jr. for helping me get back to nature in a much more profound way. I spent a week learning survival skills in New Jersey with him and his other teachers. This was going to be the last of that particular course he was going to be seen on as he was leaving his other teachers to work on this basic course. My head would have taken me back there to learn more, but in following my heart I still have not gone for more lessons on that aspect of life. The same with Arcosanti; wonderful as it was there was only one trip to

Arizona and working on the city of the future. I enjoyed my time there and made friends with the remarkable Doctress Neutopia. We spent Labor Day walking around the red rocks of Sedona and have kept up some form of correspondence ever since. Paolo Soleri was a complete inspiration, and it was a privilege to discuss philosophy with him. A year later I was in New Mexico with another extraordinary woman—Roshi Joan Halifax. I also met the very gracious Zulheikha who was there to do a dance workshop. It was with her that the roshi said we would be dancing the next day, and in the place where we were dancing there was a rainbow drawn around some artefacts that had been buried below the floor. The shock of that took time to get over, because *Dancing with the Rainbow* was the title of the book I had written some years earlier. How could I have known I was going to do exactly that five years later? Zulheikha had stopped me one day when I was gardening and told me that I was special. It was a kind thing to say, as I certainly found it hard to believe that I could be any different from anybody else. While I was there after a woman's retreat 9/11 happened, and there I was looking for the home of D. H. Lawrence when I found myself in a shaken world. I found his ranch on that famous day, which turned out also to be his birthday and the first day he had ever seen the ranch, so the synchronicity was very strong. His symbol was the phoenix rising from the ashes, and again this was seen as something America needed to do. As the country was so unstable I felt that the best thing was to go back to Sante Fe and spend more time there with the roshi. She welcomed me back, and I attended a stand for peace with her outside the Sante Fe post office. When I was there I realized that one of my great fears had been to be stuck in a foreign land at the time of war, and in a sense that is what had happened. All the

timing before that meant that is exactly where I was supposed
to be. I do meditate, but I would not call myself a Buddhist at
all. In fact I have probably been meditating for about fifteen
years if I look back.

In 2002 I found myself slightly lost again and some would
term homeless for a while. It was hard to deal with, but I
think again I needed the shaking up in some way. I thought
I had to be another way, but I had no idea really what I was
at all and what were my strengths. Slowly as I watched others
I saw that I had a lot to give. I made many friends over the
years, and it was only when I left Wales in 2002 that I noticed
just how many friends I had made there in rather a short time.
It was hard to leave, but again I needed to be somewhere else
and work on other things. I so wanted to belong, and yet my
heart seemed to say not yet all the time, keep going.

In 2003, after a short visit to Australia where I had to look
deeply at the feeling of being abandoned all over again, there
was also an incident on the plane going that helped me look at
how memory is held in the body. A curtain between the two
class areas kept rubbing my leg in the night when the stewards
walked through. This very action brought back memories
of a famous singer trying it on, hoping to have sex with me,
when I was much younger. I repeatedly said "No" to him, but
he did not hear the words. I did keep him off me but I was
covered in bruises by the morning. My whole body responded
to this memory, and I found myself feeling ill and sick on the
plane. I had to be very clear to the stewards that I needed to
move before I panicked completely. It spoiled the trip to visit
a friend, and I ended up going to California instead to a place
I had good memories of instead of bad. There I was able to
inquire into my love for the Native American traditions and
spent time looking at that and alcoholism, which had also

been a big issue in my life. Growing up in a family where my father had problems with drink I found that it kept coming back in the people I met. I have never really noticed being addicted to much; the only thing I have been aware of was that I seemed to be addicted to alcoholics in some deep effort to heal my fears regarding that issue.. There I was able to go to Al-Anon and make friends with people who understood my problems. The people in the area I stayed in were enormously kind, and that was so helpful to me. I made close friends there and still keep in touch. I was friendly with a man who had nearly died with heart problems, and through him I was able to go to two sweats at sweat lodges where I was able to see quite a lot of my own arrogance but also a lot of my own humility, both sides of the coin. They were beautiful services held by a medicine man, and I am ever grateful to him and my friends there for taking me in and allowing me to see so much about myself.

It wasn't until 2005 that I found myself again being taken on another journey of healing. I had moved close to Bradford and was living in a house of artists. I had been asked to sit on a committee for a local arts festival and wondered how I could contribute. It was then that several things came together. First of all I remember a German woman who had been in England for a short while and had been warned by her boyfriend not to go to Bradford, as it was dangerous because of the riots that had taken place sometime before. At the same time I thought of a radio interview I had heard many years earlier about a chap who called himself "The Scary Guy," and I had been in tears when I heard about his work with kids. Perhaps my thought was that I could get him to Bradford to help the children who found themselves bullied because they did not fit in due to religion and color, etc. I contacted his manager and was asked to go and see him work in Scarborough. It was a very cold March 1, St David's Day, when I took the train. I had to get up very early indeed to get there on time and had not slept well, as my friend David who slept upstairs fell in the night and woke me up and I could not get back to sleep. I suppose I was too frightened of sleeping in and wondered exactly what the bang was above me. I was intrigued by the work of "The Scary Guy" and glad to see and meet him and his wife and watch them perform and see the looks of awe and wonder on the kids' faces. Scary was very intuitive and seemed to know at lunch what I needed before I needed it. I was determined to get him to Bradford but found resistance when I started asking around from various people. I was asked to visit him again in another place that turned out to be the school I was bullied at. Originally I had not thoughts about my own bullying but was hoping to help others. I had no idea that the exercise was going to help me too. He taught hugs and love in a wonderful way. I am saddened the people of Bradford never got the chance to hear him. That night when I returned from Bradford I ended up reading some of my poetry out to friends. It started a whole new experience of performing poetry to people I did not know. I still find it hard to describe myself as a poet, but I have lots of poems as evidence that I am.

Soon after that I ended up back in California again and went to an Isadora Duncan dance workshop after going back to see the friends I had been with previously. At the time my confidence was growing. Facing a childhood dream to dance with the dancers I so admired was pretty intimidating, but on I went. In a way it was a dream come true, I had admired Isadora and her freedom to dance from the heart since the seventies. She seemed to be a remarkable woman with a clear vision and the strength to follow it. In the meantime I had been getting a better body image by dancing in England doing the Five Rhythms, designed by Gabrielle Roth. Yet there was this need to explore more about Isadora. I had read the latest biography of her and found the classes on the Internet. At first I thought I might go to New York for the experience, but it wasn't the right timing. When I saw that they were going to California I realized that I could combine seeing friends and exploring that need. I hired a car from Reno to make the journey and after seeing friends drove across California to meet them. I attended the classes but started to feel ill and uncomfortable toward the end. I had no idea that I looked like her until I later saw a couple of books with her picture in them. I have two identical pictures where we look so alike. I know I have Duncan as a surname in my family but still have not been able to trace our connections. I was asked by their PR person if I was a relative and answered "no." But this realization did not come until I arrived back in England. In some ways it was the scariest thing I have ever done, but I am glad I went. Part of the package was that you got a silk scarf. As I did not get it until later I found myself painting a picture of my bed inspired by the great artist Frida Kahlo, and in the painting I painted the silk scarf I later received by post. It was exactly the same color as in the painting! The same year I took myself to London to see my favorite flamenco dancer, Joaquin Cortes. He was performing at the Royal Albert Hall, so I treated myself to a ticket. It turned out to be on at the same weekend as the big concert in Hyde Park, and there was an exhibition of Frida at Tate Modern. I ended up having an extraordinary weekend. I went to London by train, and as I made way via Hyde Park to the Royal Albert Hall I was treated to lots of free music from the park on huge monitors. In the evening I watched Joaquin in joy as he performed beautifully Then when I left to go to the hostel I was staying in there was more music from the park, and when I got near the hostel there was a free classical concert to listen to. The next day I went to see Frida's work and then, happily exhausted, took the train home.

That was quite a year for me, as I discovered my half-sister, or she discovered us. I had a vague feeling she existed but did not want to disrupt her life. Our father had never mentioned his previous marriage or three of his sisters, so when he died these things came into the open. I had wondered for many years about the existence of a first wife, but he denied his sisters, so he certainly wasn't going to come clean about his wife. I had found things out when I was living in Wales, some by chance, as I found a document on the Internet that told of his trip to Canada indeed with a wife. I then found from his Canadian Royal Air Force records that most of his stories did not tie in with this bit of paper, so it was a shock to say the least that so much I had believed to be true was—well, what was true? I was very disinclined to shake up anybody else's life as mine had been. I was pleased to be living with the group of people who could support me when the truth finally hit me. My sister and I finally met when I came back from America at a place in England, and she and her husband had chosen it, it was where my own parents had spent their honeymoon. There was no way they could have known this fact, and even my brother was not aware that the synchronicity was happening all over again. Luck came into it again when I found out that it was not the same hotel that my parents had stayed at. By some weird chance the hotel registers from all those years ago had been kept upstairs on the top landing, so unless they had been there under assumed names there was no record of them spending their honeymoon in that hotel. It was odd to meet someone who looked just like you in so many ways. As we stood together outside the hotel for the family photo shoot, you can see the resemblance. I feel compassion for my father even so because he felt he had to live a lie, but I know I do not have to even if others wish it was different.

The next year I was looking into the Goddess culture to try to understand it better. I kept reading books but got chosen to go on a course in Glastonbury. I had sent my details, and so at the beginning of February I went to look at the Goddess Brigit. It was an interesting course, and like many others courses I have attended I seemed to fall in knowing very little about her. We had to take something for the center of the room, and I chose an acorn, not realizing that the oak was her tree. It was an enjoyable course, but I find Glastonbury difficult. It could be all the conflicting energies, I think. At the end we had a choice to pledge ourselves to Brigit. My heart told me to go all the way, and so I have by lighting a candle each Wednesday and reminding myself of her gifts. It seems a little thing to do, to remember the earth and all it gives us and let in a little light.

I had been staying with my sister before I went there and had read her some of my poetry. She wanted a copy but realized, as she was nearly blind, that it was not going to be easy for her to read it. I was wondering what I could do when I was wandering through Bradford with a friend and saw a radio station. He suggested that I should ask them if they could help. I rang the bell and entered. The person behind the desk was fascinated with my story and called some people down to meet me. They said if I would do a radio interview and talk about meeting my sister they would give me radio time to make a CD of my poetry for her. I could not believe my luck that this should happen and waited for the call to the station. It turned out to be the day another of our flock had his thirtieth birthday. He had an exhibition in Leeds Playhouse. I asked if I could say "Happy Birthday" and talk about his exhibition, and they said it was all right. How happy I was to be able to give him publicity for his excellent work. Unfortunately he is not with us any longer, as he killed himself several years later, not being able to live with himself and the disease that affected him badly. He was a lovely young man, and we all miss him.

You can imagine my joy at being able to send my sister the CD and have a copy of a lot of my writing in that format. I went back to stay with her and check out Glastonbury again later in the year and do the Spiral Dance with Starhawk. In 1996 I had read her book of the same name—a friend had recommended it—and I never imagined I would end up dancing with her and even speaking to her. From that I realized how much I had moved on and how much I had done in the intermediary years. She taught us to walk gently on the earth, something I had myself taught in Wales, and gave us healing waters of the planet, and by chance yet again the bowl was passed to me to hand out. Starhawk is a remarkable woman again who has done a lot to help the earth and stand for just causes as well as teach permaculture and the Goddess Worship. She continually puts her head above the parapet and is very brave. Yet I could not stay there and found myself driving around Dorset rather disturbed and could not find the cause of my disturbance. I ended up going home shortly after. I had moved by then to my own place to get more healing, but I did not know it at the time.

There was a very good local Al-Anon meeting close by, and so I went there regularly to deal with the fears raised

111

by the alcoholism around me. Although it often brought up painful things, with a year's therapy on top I felt that I had dealt with a lot of stuff that needed bringing out into the open and healing. I had been left some money by an aunt, and with some of it I acquired some woodland. This was very important to me as I realized that I needed wild places from time to time. This was a definite luxury to allow myself that freedom and to work in the wood alone. At last it felt like I had something I could call my own even if in reality you cannot own anything; our belongings main tendency is to own you instead. There were so many metaphors with the wood, and it soon became a place of healing for me and my friends. I had imagined many nights under canvas there, but it seemed as soon as I bought the wood the rains came and the thoughts of sleeping there was put off for now. It was a place where I could practise my Tom Brown Jr. stuff and a place to be quiet and write poetry, a joyous place with lovely views from either side of it.

I had some more interesting synchronicity when living alone in the small house with the great view, mostly through books. The biggest one happened when I went to a book festival and met Ben Okri. I had the intuition that trees were going to come into his conversation, and so when I bought his book at the end of the talk I mentioned this to him. I told him about the wood, and he was very interested. When he came to write my name in the book he kept calling me "Best." I said no I am called Bess, and so he wrote that. He called out to me as I left to look after the trees. It was that night when reading another book in bed that I again found myself shocked by the synchronicity with the two books. In the place of best in this book it said "bess." I had to photocopy it so I could remind myself I had not imagined it. So amazed was I.

Another time on the anniversary of my first wedding day I found a book that I had been looking for for a long time. It was in the window of a charity shop. I took it home only to find that the heroine was called Tess Sullivan. Sullivan had been my married name, and Tess was as near as Bess as it could be, so I was not going to forget that incident in a hurry.

I was quite enjoying living in the little market town and having my own home but was having problems with my ex-partner of many years. I had been working through Byron Katie's wonderful *The Work,* which helps you come to terms with acceptance. Somehow I had to accept my ex's behavior and still be able to give him unconditional love. It was a real test, as he was living with a woman who had a child and his stance all the years I had been with him was that he did not want children. Did he say it to make me feel better? I do not know, but we never did have children, and now he was becoming a father figure and accepting her need to smoke dope all the time. Previously he had been against drugs. I hardly knew him now, and yet he came round for reassurance, especially when they had a quarrel. He was a changed man and having blackouts from all the alcohol he was consuming. There was nothing I could do but keep attending the meetings. I will always be grateful for them and the "Serenity Prayer" that has saved so many of us. It meant I had to look at my childlessness all over again or maybe just the first time ever at that depth.

It was while I was still living there that I started to reread *Women Who Run with the Wolves.* In some ways I blame it for taking me on this splendid journey, as it was just after the first reading when I got the need to follow my intuition or heart. So I suppose I should not have been surprised that again after reading it I looked at my friend Ann's website and saw that she was going to Mexico with Tanis Helliwell and running a women's retreat. I e-mailed her to see if it would be all right for me to attend, as I knew her and sometimes trainers/ teachers prefer not to have people there they already knew. She did not have a problem with it. As I always had wanted to go to Mexico and it seemed my next step I booked a place on the course. It was going to take place the next year, so I had something to look forward to in the future. This was from a person who in the nineties identified a fear in traveling away from home, so when I initially went to Canada to meet Ann it was a really big deal for me and I was definitely moving way out of my comfort zone. The course was in late January, but just beforehand and around that Christmas I started to get a very bad cold or flu and felt more and more ill. My ex-partner was becoming and more awkward, and his behavior was getting bizarre, so I was worried about him and did not really understand what was going on with him. Well, I did on one level but not on another. In any case it was hard to operate and I hoped I would get better for my journey abroad.

I got through a very miserable period with most days in bed not able to eat and my sleeping all over the place. I was alone for long periods of time. I had just gotten to sleep on New Year's Eve when my ex-partner rang all happy and woke me to wish me "Happy New Year." The last thing I wanted was to be woken from my lovely sleep. Instead of getting back to that state I found myself awake for most of the night. The next day I decided to go and see him to try to make sense of it all and found him totally angry that I had dared do such a thing. I should have stayed in my place and not questioned any of his actions. I could not give up—I needed some sort of honesty. It was not to come, but what did happen changed my life. His best friend, seeing me so miserable and treated so badly, spoke with me about the series of events that had taken place, and in this conversation we realized that we wanted to be together and spend time. It was as if this event had been waiting years, because we spent most of the next month together—well, three weeks until I was to go to Mexico. It was such joy to be able to voice so much after so long. It was so strange. We had known each other for years and had never really seen us together, but it made sense more and more. I certainly felt as comfortable with him as I had with any other human being. In fact over three years later we are happily married. Even when we looked at our names they fit together—my surname is his first name, and his mother's name is very similar to mine in the way it is a shortened name for Elizabeth, but we were christened the shortened name and not the full name. It looks as if we were actually destined to be together.

Going to Mexico was hard not because I did not want to go but because he found out he had cancer just before I left. My question then was should I go or not? I realized that I did not want ever to have resentment in our relationship and took the plane to meet Ann and her husband Paul. I had a few days beforehand to get used to the place before I went on the retreat and nursed in my mind all the new things I had found out. While waiting in the hotel before getting on the plane he had asked me to marry him, and I knew without a doubt I was going to and that for the first time in my life I was doing the right thing. Mexico was wonderful. I loved the colors and so much about the place. Howard and I kept in touch all the time by mobile phone, and then I took a bus down the coast. Suddenly I was worried whether Ann and I would still care for each other after all those years, we had not seen each other for twelve years, but the first morning of the retreat when I met Ann I felt an overwhelming love for her and was so glad I had taken the long journey to be with her again. It was an interesting course with a lovely set of women, and we had a lot of fun. Ann's husband was the only man there, and each morning he played for us. It was a great treat, as this man is an exceptional musician and the father of New Age music. At the end of the week they gave us a private concert out in the open under the beautiful Mexican sky. I stayed on a little longer than the retreat and had some special time with both Ann and Paul, going out to dinner with them in the evening. It was a lovely time, and I will treasure it forever. It somehow gave me the strength to nurse my love through his cancer and get him to the all clear.

Looking back at pictures of him I realize just how ill he had been, but of course when you are in the middle of it, it is just about taking one day at a time. When he had the second operation I bought myself my friend Roshi Joan Halifax's book *Living with the Dying*. I needed to see what I might be facing, because the second operation was even bigger than the first in some ways. The book showed me my ego around death and was really very helpful. I have thanked Joan for that book and the wisdom it gave me. Now beside me is a healthy man who loves life and has learned so much from the time in his life when he was facing so much. In a sense I feel that it deepened our relationship, because when you are faced with something life threatening that there can be little ego there, and so we did not waste time; we had to be truthful with each other. Not possibly the most romantic way to start a relationship!

In the course of the healing we moved to the country and soon had hens and a quiet life except for the busy road close by, but we did not notice it at first. The move to the country was meant to get us closer to Mother, who was going downhill fast. The day we moved into the cottage was her birthday, and by then she had had a stroke and it was clear she was not going to be able to go home. By the time I was moving I had two houses to clean—hers and mine. It was a stressful time, and we decided that Mum would be better off in Cumbria near my brother, as he had a bigger family to visit and she now had few friends in the area where she lived, most having left us because of their and her great age. The result of all this is we visited Cumbria more often and got to know parts of Scotland that we would have possibly not visited if she had stayed in Yorkshire. We stayed in a variety of places—sometimes camping, sometimes in a bed and breakfast place, and sometimes a hotel. By the time I was sixty she did not really know who I was, so these painful visits were helped by our staying nearby. On one holiday we came across a lovely hotel that seemed to call me. When we got there a man asked us to his art exhibition. I told him we were going home that day, so he asked us to come the next day to see it before it was open to the public. We agreed and decided to have lunch at the hotel. The owner took us round the hotel, and we vowed to come back. With the lovely lunch, the art, and the total ambience we were hooked. It stood in its own grounds and looked over the sea. There was something very special about it for us. Later we visited the Isle of Mull and again found a wonderful peace about the place that we did not have at home, so we decided initially to look for a new home in Scotland. That of course did not happen, but what did come out of those journeys was that we got married in the hotel when I was sixty-one and Howard was sixty. It was a wonderful wedding even though very small, and by that time we had the gorgeous Honey by our side. The clothes I wore for the occasion were all picked by intuition. The dress was the first one I tried on, and I knew it was the one. The shoes were there waiting for me when I visited York with a friend. Everything just fell into place, and I had not one doubt again that I was doing the right thing. The owner of the hotel was marvelous and kind, and when we got there we found that we had the whole place to ourselves. If we had tried to book a whole hotel for our wedding it would have cost a fortune, but in our case it just worked out perfectly. Our friends were very supportive, and we will always remember them and the day with tenderness.

Mother eventually died. In fact she died just before we got married and came in spirit form to make everything right between us. It was four in the morning, and I am clear that is what happened, as I have been aware of spirits beforehand. I was not expecting her, but when she came there was peace between us. It was a lovely thing to happen and gave me the freedom from thinking I am not enough. I think it was that sense of freedom that gave us the chance to move onto this journey. All the time I lived at the cottage I noticed how I was growing and losing so much of the upset of the past. All my hard work was paying off at last. The upsets that touch my ego became smaller and smaller, thank goodness, and I could start to have more compassion for others in dark places.

What did help through the years, though, was meditation, taking better care of myself, my gratitude diary and journaling, walking in the countryside, dancing, painting, writing, and affirmations. They all helped my stress levels bit by bit. I have used Louise Hay's affirmations for years now, and they have helped me review myself.

I realize that I have given an awful lot of information in a small space, as so much happened over those years and with so much more detail that it would take several books to write it all down. Yet I feel that I have given you the key facts of this, what seems to be a modern pilgrimage. Perhaps now I can call myself an earth pilgrim, or traveler with husband and a small dog. It was well worth it, and as I sit in this wonderful farmhouse with an orchard to marvel at I know I would do it all again if asked. It was well worth doing it even though very hard going at times. What could be more pleasing than that?

Gratitudes

The first book to inspire me to go deeper was by Clarissa Pinkola Estes and was called Women *Who Run with the Wolves*. This book inspired me on my first big journey to Canada.

I then read *The Spiral Dance* by Starhawk.

A handy little book to take on your travels is Susan Jeffers's *The Little Book of Peace*, but I probably would not have traveled at all if I had not read her *Feel the Fear and Do It Anyway*.

Most of the affirmations I have used come from Louise Hay's *Heal your Body*.

I learned about Tom Brown Jr. from his book *Grandfather* and then went on to read many more of his books, including *The Vision*.

In 1998 I bought a second-hand copy of Carolyn Mary Keefeld's *Alchemy of Possibility*. It had been owned by Ram Dass. It has been an inspiring book, especially when I am stuck and do not understand something. All I have to do is open up and somehow that page has my answer.

When I started to do the Five Rhythms I bought Gabrielle Roth's book *Maps to Ecstasy*. It helped me understand each rhythm. I got to dance with Gabrielle in London when she was hosting a charity event.

Another very useful book is Eckhart Tolle's *The Power of Now* and then later *The New Earth*. He talked about this book with Oprah, and like so many I have deep gratitude for Oprah in introducing us to so much. I am not sure I would have started my gratitude journal if it had not been for her.

Byron Katie also has given us *The Work*, a brilliant way to get more acceptances in your life. I have read several of her books.

I saw *The Vagina Monologues* for the first time in Wales and have seen it several times in other areas of the country. Eve Ensler's *Insecure at Last* got me through one Christmas. She is a real hero for all she has done in the world.

Kathy Jones has written a variety of books about the Goddess. Of those I have read *Spinning the Wheel of Ana* and *The Ancient British Goddess*.

Oriah Mountain Dreamer's poem "The Invitation" is given out by the Scary Guy when he does his talk. I have read nearly all her books.

Satish Kumar originally wrote *No Destination* about his peace walks, but since then I have read his *You Are, Therefore I Am*, a declaration of independence, and his *Earth Pilgrim*.

On this journey I had with me Ann Mortifee's *In Love with the Mystery*, Jean Houston's *The Hero and the Goddess*, Roshi Joan Halifax's *Fruitful Darkness*, *Connecting with the Body of the Earth*, and Paoli Soleri's *Arcosanti, an Urban Laboratory*.

Some of the books of fiction that I have mentioned are Ben Okri's *Starbook* and Alice Walker's *By the Light of My Father's Smile*. There were also *The Mermaid Chair* by Sue Monk Kidd and *The Lucana* by Barbara Kingsolver. And of course there is special gratitude to Aldous Huxley and D. H. Lawrence for all their work and to Isadora (books *Isadora: A Sensational Life* by Peter Kurth; and *Isadora Speaks,* writings, and speeches by Isadora).

I apologize for any book I have not mentioned here. I might have just missed out one or two.

WOOD

I look between the gaps
At the empty spaces
Each tree a separate unit
But together they make the forest.
There is a distance between us now
Your image is still on my retina
But a mirror reflects you back to me
And brings you closer
Together we make a family
The beech becomes part of it too
As does the wren in the leaf litter
And the small dog on the back seat.